D1542590

Bible. English. Selections. 1979.

Bible for Today

DISCARD

Library Of
TRINITY LUTHERAN SEMINARY
2199 E. Main St.
Columbus, Ohio 43209

THE WESTMINSTER PRESS
PHILADELPHIA

Juv
BS
391.2
.W42

I. A Nation encounters God

As long as there have been people on the earth, they have been asking questions. They have been looking for answers to the mysteries of life: Why are we alive? – Where do we come from? – Where are we going? – Who will lead us? – How should we live? – Is there a meaning in life?

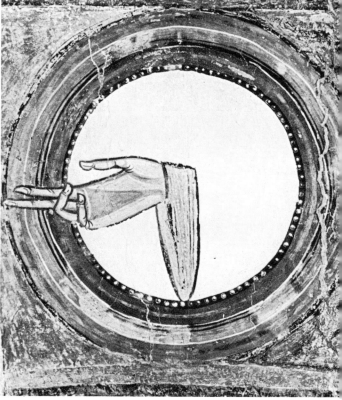

11-5-80

T-6030

Whenever we ask such questions as these, we also talk about God. We did not invent God, or decide for ourselves where he lives and who he is. God has actually shown himself to us. He came in the person of Jesus. In Jesus we have seen how God is related to us and what he does for us.

In fact many hundreds of years before Jesus was born, God began to have dealings with people and to show himself to them. To do this he picked out one nation in particular: Israel. So the story of God's dealings with us begins with the Israelites. As time went on, Israel discovered that God was with them and cared about everything that happened to them.

The Israelites told many stories of their adventures with God. At first these stories were handed on by word of mouth, but later they were brought together and written down. The result was 'the Scriptures of Israel', which we call the Old Testament.

The Scriptures of the Old Testament tell us about the normal events of everyday living – birth and death, people's laughter and their tears, the good they do and also the bad. The stories demonstrate how God is involved in everything that happens, and they show what part he plays in people's lives.

The Old Testament also gives us answers to our own questions today. It can help us to find God and share our lives with him. Only when we have understood Israel's main encounters with God can we go on to understand what the New Testament has to say about Jesus.

God was not invented by men   1

Before you created the hills
or brought the world into being,
you were eternally God,
and will be God for ever.

Psalm 90:2

1. The God who cannot be comprehended

When Israel first came to know God, its people still worshipped many different gods. Each tribe, and even each family, would have its own god. There were gods for war, for rain, for animals, and in fact for anything that the people considered important. They liked to possess their god – it belonged to them. So they would often make an image out of wood or stone and call it a god. Then they would build a magnificent temple and say that that was where their god lived.

At first the Israelites also thought of their God as one among many. But God told them that he was different from other people's gods. They were idols, not really gods – he alone was God. They were made by people, whereas he was the one who made us. He was far greater and more holy than they could possibly imagine. No one could comprehend him, or take hold of him and possess him. God is not at our disposal, because he is the God who cannot be comprehended.

God cannot be compared with anything 2

Lord God Almighty,
none is as mighty as you;
in all things you are faithful,
O Lord.

You rule over the powerful sea;
you calm its angry waves.
Psalm 89:8–9

God's thoughts are not ours 3

'My thoughts,' says the Lord,
'are not like yours,
and my ways are different from yours.

As high as the heavens are above the earth,
so high are my ways and thoughts above yours.'
Isaiah 55:8–9

God is like a riddle 4

O God, how difficult I find your thoughts;
how many of them there are!

If I counted them,
they would be more than the grains of sand.
Psalm 139:17–18

God may not be seen

Then Moses requested, 'Please, let me see the dazzling light of your presence.'

The LORD answered, 'I will make all my splendour pass before you and in your presence I will pronounce my sacred name. I am the LORD, and I show compassion and pity on those I choose. I will not let you see my face, because no one can see me and stay alive, but here is a place beside me where you can stand on a rock. When the dazzling light of my presence passes by, I will put you in an opening in the rock and cover you with my hand until I have passed by.

Then I will take my hand away, and you will see my back but not my face.'

Exodus 33:18–23

6 No one is like God

Can anyone measure the ocean by handfuls
   or measure the sky with his hands?

Can anyone hold the soil of the earth in
   a cup or weigh the mountains and hills
   on scales?

To the LORD the nations are nothing,
   no more than a drop of water;
   the distant islands are as light as dust.

The nations are nothing at all to him.

To whom can God be compared?
How can you describe what he is like?
Isaiah 40:12,15,17,18

You rule over the powerful sea;
  you calm its angry waves.
Heaven is yours, the earth also;
  you made the world and everything in it.
You created the north and the south;
How powerful you are!
How great is your strength!
Your kingdom is founded
  on righteousness and justice;
  love and faithfulness are shown
  in all you do.
How happy are the people
  who worship you with songs,
  who live in the light of your kindness!
Because of you they rejoice all day long,
  and they praise you for your goodness.
You give us great victories;
  in your love you make us triumphant.
From Psalm 89:9–17

2. God has set us free

A most important time for the Israelites was when they left the land of Egypt. They were oppressed and treated very badly there. They had to work for the Egyptians like imprisoned servants or slaves.

It was a man called Moses who led the Israelites out of Egypt. After a long journey through the desert they came to the land of Canaan. Once they were released from the slavery of the Egyptians, and all through their long journey across the desert, they came to realize that the one who had actually saved them and led them out was God. He was a God who set people free.

Israel went on telling of their adventures with God. Through many prayers and stories they remembered how God had set them free, and they were thankful.

8 | **This our God has done**

My ancestor was a wandering shepherd,
who took his family to Egypt to live.
They were few in number when they went
there, but they became a large and powerful
nation.

The Egyptians treated us harshly
and forced us to work as slaves.
Then we cried out for help to the LORD,
the God of our ancestors.

He heard us and saw our suffering,
hardship, and misery.
By his great power and strength
he rescued us from Egypt.
He worked miracles and wonders,
and caused terrifying things to happen.

He brought us here
and gave us this rich and fertile land.
From Deuteronomy 26:5–9

9 I am who I am

The Israelites were groaning under their slavery and cried out for help. Their cry went up to God, who heard their groaning and remembered his covenant with Abraham, Isaac, and Jacob.

One day while Moses was taking care of the sheep and goats of his father-in-law Jethro, the priest of Midian, he led the flock across the desert and came to Sinai, the holy mountain. There the angel of the LORD appeared to him as a flame coming from the middle of a bush. Moses saw that the bush was on fire but that it was not burning up. When the LORD saw that Moses was coming closer, he called to him from the middle of the bush and said, 'Moses! Moses!'
He answered, 'Yes, here I am.'
God said, 'Do not come any closer. Take off your sandals, because you are standing on holy ground. I am the God of your ancestors, the God of Abraham, Isaac, and Jacob. I have seen how cruelly my people are being treated in Egypt. I know all about their sufferings, and so I have come down to rescue them from the Egyptians and to bring them out of Egypt to a spacious land, one which is rich and fertile. Now I am sending you to the king of Egypt so that you can lead my people out of his country.'
But Moses replied, 'When I go to the Israelites, they will ask me your name. So what can I tell them?'

God said, 'I am who I am. This is what you must say to them: "The one who is called I AM has sent me to you."

'Tell the Israelites that I, the LORD, the God of their ancestors, the God of Abraham, Isaac, and Jacob, have sent you to them. This is my name for ever; this is what all future generations are to call me.
'I have decided that I will bring them out of Egypt, where they are being treated cruelly, and will take them to a rich and fertile land.'
From Exodus 2:23–24; 3:1–17

10 God has saved us

When the king of Egypt was told that the people had escaped, he got his war chariot and his army ready. He set out with all his chariots, including the six hundred finest, commanded by their officers. When the Israelites saw the king and his army marching against them, they were terrified and cried out to the LORD for help.

Moses said, 'Don't be afraid! Stand your ground, and you will see what the LORD will do to save you today.'

The angel of God, who had been in front of the army of Israel, moved and went to the rear. A pillar of cloud also moved until it was between the Egyptians and the Israelites.

Moses held out his hand over the sea, and the LORD drove the sea back with a strong east wind. The water was divided, and the Israelites went through the sea on dry ground, with walls of water on both sides. The Egyptians went after them into the sea with all their horses, chariots, and drivers. Moses held out his hand over the sea, and the water returned and covered all the Egyptian army that had followed the Israelites into the sea.

When the Israelites saw the great power with which the LORD had defeated the Egyptians, they feared the LORD; and they had faith in the LORD and in his servant Moses.

From Exodus 14

1 The song of victory at the Red Sea

I will sing to the LORD,
because he has won a glorious victory.

The LORD is my strong defender;
he is the one who has saved me.

He is my God,
and I will praise him,
my father's God,
and I will sing about his greatness.

The LORD is a warrior;
the LORD is his name.

Your right hand, LORD, is awesome in power;
it breaks the enemy in pieces.
They sank like lead in the terrible water.

LORD, who among the gods is like you?
Who is like you, wonderful in holiness?
Who can work miracles and mighty acts like
yours?

Faithful to your promise,
you led the people you had rescued;
by your strength
you guided them to your sacred land.

From Exodus 15:1–13

3. He is with us

During the long journey in the desert after they had left Egypt, and again later in the land of Canaan, the Israelites grew to learn what the name of the Lord meant, which Moses had given them: God is with us. He cares for us. He looks after us as a good shepherd looks after his flock. There are many stories in the Old Testament which give examples of this.

12 He cares about us

The whole Israelite community set out, and in the desert they all complained to Moses, 'We wish that the LORD had killed us in Egypt. There we could at least sit down and eat meat and as much other food as we wanted. But you have brought us out into this desert to starve us all to death.' The LORD said to Moses, 'Now I am going to make food rain down from the sky for all of you.' So Moses said to all the Israelites, 'This evening you will know that it was the LORD who brought you out of Egypt. The LORD will give you meat to eat in the evening and as much bread as you want in the morning.'
In the evening a large flock of quails flew in, enough to cover the camp, and in the morning there was dew all round the camp. When the dew evaporated, there was something thin and flaky on the surface of the desert. It was as delicate as frost. When the Israelites saw it, they didn't know what it was and asked each other, 'What is it?' Moses said to them, 'This is the food that the LORD has given you to eat.'
From Exodus 16:1–15

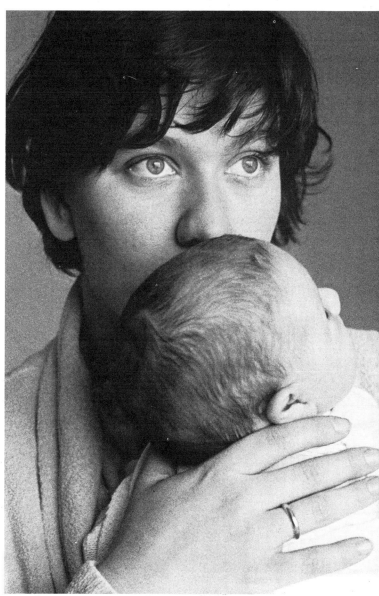

3 God is like a father

As kind as a father is to his children,
so kind is the Lord to those who honour him.
For those who honour the Lord,
his love lasts for ever,
and his goodness endures for all generations
of those who are true to his covenant
and who faithfully obey his commands.

Psalm 103:13,17–18

4 God is like a mother

Can a woman forget her own baby
and not love the child she bore?
Even if a mother should forget her child,
I will never forget you.

Isaiah 49:15

God is like a shepherd

The Sovereign LORD is coming to rule with power, bringing with him the people he has rescued. He will take care of his flock like a shepherd; he will gather the lambs together and carry them in his arms;
he will gently lead their mothers.

Isaiah 40:10–11

The LORD is my shepherd;
I have everything I need.
He lets me rest in fields of green grass
and leads me to quiet pools of fresh water.

Even if I go through the deepest darkness,
I will not be afraid, LORD,
for you are with me.

Psalm 23:1–2,4

4. A covenant with God

During the journey across the desert, on Mount Sinai, something very significant happened: God and the people of Israel made a covenant. This meant that they joined themselves to each other. God joined himself to the Israelites, and they were to be joined to him. He chose them as his own possession. They were to belong to him alone and they had to do what he wanted. As long as they kept the covenant, all would be well.

I will be your God   17

I will keep my part of the covenant
that I made with you.
I will live among you in my sacred tent,
and I will never turn away from you.
I will be with you;
I will be your God,
and you will be my people.
Leviticus 26:9,11–12

You will be my people   18

On the first day of the third month after they had left Egypt they came to the desert of Sinai. There they set up camp at the foot of Mount Sinai, and Moses went up the mountain to meet with God.

The LORD called to him from the mountain and told him to say to the Israelites, Jacob's descendants:

'You saw what I, the LORD, did to the Egyptians and how I carried you as an eagle carries her young on her wings, and brought you here to me. Now, if you will obey me and keep my covenant, you will be my own people. The whole earth is mine, but you will be my chosen people, a people dedicated to me alone.'

So Moses went down and told them everything that the LORD had commanded him. Then all the people answered together, 'We will do everything that the LORD has said.'
From Exodus 19:1–8

19 You will have all you want

The LORD your God is bringing you into a fertile
land –
a land that has rivers and springs,
and underground streams
gushing out into the valleys and hills;
a land that produces wheat and barley,
grapes, figs, pomegranates, olives, and honey.
There you will never go hungry
or ever be in need.
Its rocks have iron in them,
and from its hills you can mine copper.
You will have all you want to eat,
and you will give thanks to the LORD your God
for the fertile land that he has given you.
Deuteronomy 8:7–10

20 You have given us everything

O LORD, my God, how great you are!

You make springs flow in the valleys,
    and rivers run between the hills,
They provide water for the wild animals.
In the trees near by,
    the birds make their nests and sing.

From the sky you send rain on the hills.
You make grass grow for the cattle
    and plants for man to use,
    so that he can grow his crops
    and produce wine to make him happy,
    and bread to give him strength.

Praise the LORD my soul!
From Psalm 104

Chosen because he loves us 21

From all the peoples on earth
he chose you to be his own special people.

The LORD did not love you and choose you
because you outnumbered other peoples;
you were the smallest nation on earth.

But the LORD loved you
and wanted to keep the promise
that he made to your ancestors.

Remember that the LORD your God
is the only God
and that he is faithful.
He will keep his covenant
and show his constant love
to a thousand generations
of those who love him
and obey his commands.
Deuteronomy 7:6–9

5. From the beginning

Many of Israel's stories tell of Abram (later called Abraham), Isaac, and Jacob and his twelve sons. The Israelites said that they were descended from these men. As their forefathers, they had believed in the same God and known him in their lives.

Therefore men in the court of King Solomon collected and wrote down the old stories that had been handed down for centuries. They wanted to show the people of Israel how it all began, how God chose their nation from the very beginning, so that one day he might be close to men and women the world over. Some of the stories showed how Abraham put his complete trust in God. This was how Israel too should put its trust in God.

22 The LORD said to Abram, 'Leave your native land, your relatives, and your father's home, and go to a country that I am going to show you. I will give you many descendants, and they will become a great nation. I will bless you and make your name famous, so that you will be a blessing.'

When Abram was seventy-five years old, he started out from Haran, as the LORD had told him to do.

From Genesis 12:1–4

The LORD said to Abram, 'From where you are, **23** look carefully in all directions. I am going to give you and your descendants all the land that you see, and it will be yours for ever. I am going to give you so many descendants that no one will be able to count them all; it would be as easy to count all the specks of dust on earth! Now, go and look over the whole land, because I am going to give it all to you.'

So Abram moved his camp and settled near the sacred trees of Mamre at Hebron, and there he built an altar to the LORD.

Genesis 13:14–18

24 Abram had a vision and heard the LORD say to him, 'Do not be afraid, Abram. I will shield you from danger and give you a great reward.' But Abram answered, 'Sovereign LORD, what good will your reward do me, since I have no children, and one of my slaves will inherit my property.'

Then he heard the LORD speaking to him again: 'This slave will not inherit your property; your own son will be your heir.' The LORD took him outside and said, 'Look at the sky and try to count the stars; you will have as many descendants as that.'

Abram put his trust in the LORD, and because of this the LORD was pleased with him and accepted him.

Genesis 15:1–6

25 When Abram was ninety-nine years old, the LORD appeared to him and said, 'I will make my covenant with you and give you many descendants, and some of them will be kings.

'I will keep my promise to you and to your descendants in future generations as an everlasting covenant. I will be your God and the God of your descendants.

The whole land of Canaan will belong to your descendants for ever, and I will be their God.'

Genesis 17:1–8

26 The LORD appeared to Abraham at the sacred trees of Mamre. As Abraham was sitting at the entrance of his tent during the hottest part of the day, he looked up and saw three men standing there. As soon as he saw them, he ran out to meet them. Bowing down with his face touching the ground, he said, 'Sirs, please do not pass by my home without stopping. I will bring a bit of food.'

Abraham hurried into the tent and said to Sarah, 'Quick, take a sack of your best flour, and bake some bread.' Then he ran to the herd and picked out a calf that was tender and fat. He took some cream, some milk, and the meat, and set the food before the men. There under the tree he served them himself, and they ate.

Then they asked him, 'Where is your wife Sarah?' 'She is there in the tent,' he answered.

One of them said, 'Nine months from now I will come back, and your wife Sarah will have a son.' Sarah was behind him, at the door of the tent, listening. Abraham and Sarah were very old, and she laughed to herself and said, 'Now that I am old and worn out, can I still enjoy sex? And besides, my husband is old too.'

Then the LORD asked Abraham, 'Why did Sarah laugh? Is anything too hard for the LORD? As I said, nine months from now I will return, and Sarah will have a son.'

Then the men left.

From Genesis 18:1–16

The LORD blessed Sarah, as he had promised, and **27** she became pregnant and bore a son to Abraham when he was old. The boy was born at the time God had said he would be born. Abraham named him Isaac. Abraham was a hundred years old when Isaac was born. Sarah said, 'God has brought me joy and laughter. Everyone who hears about it will laugh with me.' Then she added, 'Who would have said to Abraham that Sarah would nurse children?'

From Genesis 21:1–7

I will not leave you

Many stories were told of a man called Jacob. Later he was called Israel. He was one of the forefathers of the people, just like Abraham and Isaac. It was from him that the nation of Israel took its name. The following two stories are pictures – as Jacob is a picture representing the whole nation – by means of which the Israelites wanted to show what they had learnt about God over the generations: God had blessed their nation; he had given them a land to live in; and he had not left them on their own.

28 Jacob came to a holy place and camped there. He lay down to sleep, resting his head on a stone. He dreamt that he saw a stairway reaching from earth to heaven, with angels going up and coming down on it. And there was the LORD standing beside him. 'I am the LORD, the God of Abraham and Isaac,' he said. 'I will give to you and to your descendants this land on which you are lying. They will be as numerous as the specks of dust on the earth. Remember, I will be with you and protect you wherever you go. I will not leave you.' Jacob woke up and said, 'The LORD is here! He is in this place, and I didn't know it!'

Jacob got up early next morning, took the stone that was under his head, and set it up as a memorial. He named the place Bethel (which means 'house of God').

Genesis 28:10–19

29 Jacob got up, took his two wives, his two concubines, and his eleven children, and crossed the River Jabbok. After he had sent them across, he also sent across all that he owned, but he stayed behind, alone.

Then a man came and wrestled with him until just before daybreak. When the man saw that he was not winning the struggle, he struck Jacob on the hip, and it was thrown out of joint. The man said, 'Let me go; daylight is coming.'

'I won't, unless you bless me,' Jacob answered.

'What is your name?' the man asked.

'Jacob,' he answered.

The man said, 'Your name will no longer be Jacob. You have struggled with God and with men, and you have won; so your name will be Israel ("God struggles").' Then he blessed Jacob.

From Genesis 32:22–30

6. It is what God wants

The Israelites had learned again and again that God was with them, that he was devoted to them. When they walked his paths, they prospered.

On Mount Sinai God had made a covenant with his people. He had promised that he would always be with them, protecting them and allowing them to live in happiness in the promised land.

What did God want of his people?

He wanted them to put him first in their lives, to love him, not to turn their backs on him and worship strange gods. Therefore Moses and the prophets continually warned Israel to remain faithful to the covenant with God and to do what God wanted.

To be joined to God in a covenant should always have an effect on living with other people: because God puts people first, they must put each other first. Because he is just and good, they should be just and good to each other. And so we find a lot of instructions in the Old Testament for living alongside other people.

These instructions show that the Lord, the God of Israel, wants the best for all mankind.

The LORD alone

Israel, remember this! The LORD – and the LORD alone – is our God. Love the LORD your God with all your heart, with all your soul, and with all your strength.

Deuteronomy 6:4–5

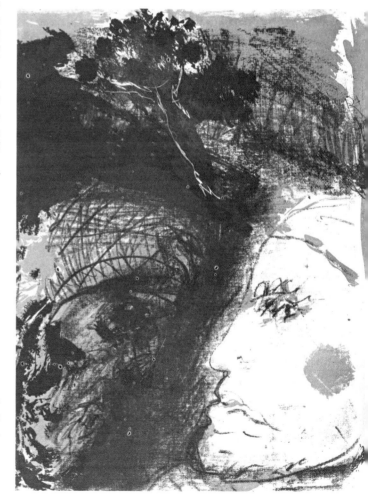

What God demands

Now, people of Israel, listen to what the LORD your God demands of you: Worship the LORD and do all that he commands. Love him, serve him with all your heart, and obey all his laws.

Deuteronomy 10:12–13

The Lord said, 'I am the LORD your God, who rescued you from Egypt, where you were slaves.

Worship no god but me.
Do not make for yourselves images of anything in heaven or on earth or in the water under the earth. Do not bow down to any idol or worship it.

Do not use my name for evil purposes, for I, the LORD your God, will punish anyone who misuses my name.

Observe the Sabbath and keep it holy. You have six days in which to do your work, but the seventh day is a day of rest dedicated to me. Your slaves must rest just as you do.

Respect your father and your mother, so that you may live a long time in the land that I am giving you.

Do not commit murder.

Do not commit adultery.

Do not steal.

Do not accuse anyone falsely.

Do not desire another man's wife;

Do not desire his house, or anything else that he owns.'

From Deuteronomy 5:6–21

When you harvest your fields, do not cut the corn at the edges of the fields, and do not go back to cut the ears of the corn that were left, leave them for poor people and foreigners. I am the LORD your God.
Do not steal or cheat or lie. Do not hold back the wages of someone you have hired. I am the LORD your God. Do not take revenge on anyone or continue to hate him, but love your neighbour as you love yourself. I am the LORD.

From Leviticus 19:9–18

34 Like a son to the Most High

My son,
do not refuse the poor a livelihood.
Do not add to the sufferings of the hungry,
do not bait a man in distress.

Do not aggravate a heart already angry,
nor keep the destitute
waiting for your alms.

Do not avert your eyes from the destitute,
give no man occasion to curse you.

Be like a father to orphans.
And you will be like a son
to the Most High,
whose love for you
will surpass your mother's.
From Ecclesiasticus 4:1–11

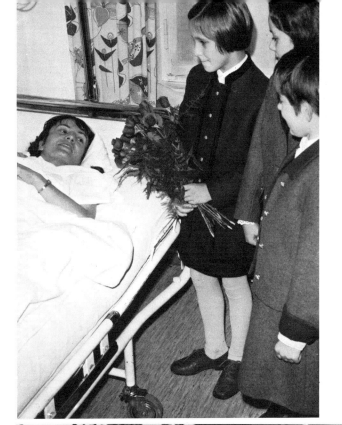

35

Long life comes to him
who honours his father,
he who sets his mother at ease
is showing obedience to the Lord.
He serves his parents
as he does his Lord.
Respect your father
in deed as well as word.
From Ecclesiasticus 3:6–8

Library Of
TRINITY LUTHERAN SEMINARY
2199 E. Main St.
Columbus, Ohio 43209

T-6030

7. God's world is for you

Eventually the Israelites settled in the land of Canaan. They knew that God had given them the land because they were his people and they had a covenant with him. And so in songs and prayers they thanked their God for the beautiful country, for the springs and brooks, the meadows and fields, the animals and the fruit on the trees. They could see that everything came from God. Just as he was there for them, so was the country too. As time went on, however, God revealed something more to the Israelites: he was not only the God of their nation; he was the God and Lord of all people.

He loves everyone in the world, for everyone in the world is his creature. So too is every thing in the world: not only human beings and animals, but also the mountains and seas, and the sun, moon and stars in the sky – everything comes from God. He created it all, and has given it to men and women. So the Israelites praised their God as the creator of every human being and of the whole universe.

Praise the Lord! 36

Praise the LORD!
Praise him, sun and moon;
praise him, shining stars.
Praise him, highest heavens,
and the waters above the sky.
Praise the LORD from the earth,
sea-monsters and all ocean depths;
lightning and hail, snow and clouds,
strong winds that obey his command.
Praise him, hills and mountains,
fruit-trees and forests;
all animals, tame and wild,
reptiles and birds.
Praise him, kings and all peoples,
princes and all other rulers;
girls and young men,
old people and children too.
Let them all praise the name of the LORD!
From Psalm 148

To govern the world 37

God of our ancestors, Lord of mercy, who by your
word have made all things, and in your wisdom
have fitted man to govern the world in holiness
and justice, grant me Wisdom, and do not reject
me from the number of your children.
From Wisdom 9:1-4

8. God is our king

38 | **How great you are**

O Lord, our Lord,
your greatness is seen
in all the world!

When I look at the sky,
which you have made,
at the moon and the stars,
which you set in their places –
what is man,
that you think of him;
mere man,
that you care for him?

You appointed him ruler
over everything you made;
you placed him over all creation:
sheep and cattle, and the wild animals too;
the birds and the fish
and the creatures in the seas.

O Lord, our Lord,
your greatness is seen
in all the world!
From Psalm 8

The Israelites spent the first two hundred years in Canaan without a king of their own. Whenever the people asked for one, the prophets would say: 'You do not need a king as the other nations do. You belong to God. God himself is your king, and he alone should rule over you.' Nevertheless the Israelites did have kings of their own later on. The first three were Saul, David and Solomon. Yet they were very different from the kings of the other nations in those days. In the other nations the king was the supreme ruler, and the people had to do anything he wanted. The king had no equal, and was often worshipped as a god.

In Israel, however, things were different. The supreme king was God himself. The kings of Israel had to obey him and see to it that the people lived according to his will.

We are told of many Israelite kings in the Old Testament. Some ruled just as God wanted them to, and so they and the people prospered. But many kings turned away from the Lord and followed their own desires. Because of this, disaster would often befall the nation.

There are many stories in the Old Testament about King David in particular. When he was on the throne Israel was a great and powerful kingdom, with Jerusalem as its capital. The following stories were to show that the Israelite kings did not rule by their own authority, but were chosen by God and ruled under his direction.

David came from the small town of Bethlehem. He was the youngest son of the sheep-owner Jesse, and with his brothers he watched over his father's sheep. One day God sent the prophet Samuel to Bethlehem. He was to make known and anoint the one whom God had chosen as the coming king of Israel.
Samuel invited Jesse and his sons to a meal.

When they arrived, Samuel saw Jesse's son Eliab and said to himself, 'This man standing here in the LORD's presence is surely the one he has chosen.' But the LORD said to him, 'Pay no attention to how tall and handsome he is. I have rejected him, because I do not judge as man judges. Man looks at the outward appearances, but I look at the heart.'
Jesse brought seven of his sons to Samuel. And Samuel said to him, 'No, the LORD hasn't chosen any of these.' Then he asked him, 'Have you any more sons?'
Jesse answered, 'There is still the youngest, but he is out taking care of the sheep.'
'Tell him to come here,' Samuel said. 'We won't eat our meal until he comes.' So Jesse sent for him. He was a handsome, healthy young man, and his eyes sparkled. The LORD said to Samuel, 'This is the one – anoint him!' Samuel took the olive-oil and anointed David in front of his brothers. Immediately the spirit of the LORD took control of David and was with him from that day on.
From I Samuel 16:6–13

40 The king: a 'son of God'

A king of Israel was often called a 'son of God'. That meant that the king belonged to God. Everything he had came from God. He did not rule with his own authority, but with the authority God had given him.

'I will announce,' says the king,
'what the LORD has declared.'
He said to me:
'You are my son;
today I have become your father.'

Now listen to this warning, you kings;
Serve the LORD with fear;
tremble and bow down to him;
or else his anger will be quickly aroused,
and you will suddenly die.
Happy are all who go to him for protection.
From a king's song—Psalm 2:7,10–12

41 In the name of the God of Israel

The Philistines gathered for battle. They lined up on one hill and the Israelites on another, with a valley between them.

A man named Goliath came out from the Philistine camp to challenge the Israelites. He was nearly three metres tall and wore bronze armour and a bronze helmet. His spear was as thick as the bar on a weaver's loom, and its iron head weighed about seven kilogrammes.

Goliath stood and shouted at the Israelites, 'Choose one of your men to fight me. If he wins and kills me, we will be your slaves; but if I win and kill him, you will be our slaves.' When Saul and his men heard this, they were terrified.

Jesse's three eldest sons had gone with Saul to war. David went to his brothers, and asked how they were getting on.

David then said to Saul, 'Your Majesty, no one should be afraid of this Philistine! I will go and fight him.'

'No,' answered Saul. 'How could you fight him? You're just a boy, and he has been a soldier all his life!'

'Your Majesty,' David said, 'The LORD has saved me from lions and bears; he will save me from this Philistine.'

'All right,' Saul answered. 'Go, and the LORD be with you.' He gave his own armour to David for him to wear. David strapped Saul's sword over the armour and tried to walk, but he couldn't, because he wasn't used to wearing them. So he took it all off. He took his shepherd's stick and then picked up five smooth stones from the stream and put them in his bag. With his catapult ready, he went out to meet Goliath.

The Philistine started walking towards David. When he got a good look at David, he was filled with scorn for him because he was just a nice, good-looking boy. He said to David, 'What's that stick for? Do you think I'm a dog?'

David answered, 'You are coming against me with sword, spear, and javelin, but I come against you in the name of the LORD Almighty, the God of the Israelite armies, which you have defied.'

Goliath started walking towards David again, and David put his hand into his bag and took out a stone, which he slung at Goliath. It hit him on the forehead and broke his skull, and Goliath fell face downwards on the ground.

When the Philistines saw that their hero was dead, they ran away.
From 1 Samuel 17

One day, late in the afternoon, David went to the palace roof. He saw a woman having a bath. She was very beautiful. He learnt that she was Bathsheba, the wife of Uriah the Hittite. David sent messengers to fetch her; they brought her to him and he made love to her.

The next morning David wrote a letter to Joab and sent it by Uriah. He wrote: 'Put Uriah in the front line, where the fighting is heaviest, then retreat and let him be killed.' But the LORD was not pleased with what David had done.

The LORD sent the prophet Nathan to David. Nathan went to him and said, 'There were two men who lived in the same town; one was rich and the other poor. The rich man had many cattle and sheep, while the poor man had only one lamb, which he had bought. He took care of it, and it grew up in his home with his children. One day a visitor arrived at the rich man's home. The rich man didn't want to kill one of his own animals to prepare a meal for him; instead, he took the poor man's lamb and cooked a meal for his guest.' David was very angry with the rich man and said, 'I swear by the living LORD that the man who did this ought to die! For having done such a cruel thing, he must pay back four times as much as he took.'

'You are that man,' Nathan said to David. 'And this is what the LORD God of Israel says: "Why have you disobeyed my commands? Why did you do this evil thing? You had Uriah killed in battle, and then you took his wife! Now, in every generation some of your descendants will die a violent death because you have disobeyed me."'

From 2 Samuel 11 and 12

9. Return to God

From the very beginning the Israelites had always had plenty to learn from their God. He had chosen them as his people and had made a covenant with them. In spite of this they did not live as the people of God should. They did not keep the covenant, nor do what God wanted. They repeatedly forgot him, turning away from him and falling back into the worship of idols.

There arose certain men – called prophets – who called the people back to God. They spoke in the name of God, but the Israelites would not listen to them. In short, they would not listen to God. Many of the prophets were rejected and persecuted. They had to suffer because they would not tell the people what they wanted to hear, but what God had commanded them to say. In the end the warnings of the prophets came true: foreign nations, the Assyrians and the Babylonians, conquered the land and led the people into captivity.

43 You have turned your backs

The children I brought up have rebelled against me. Cattle know who owns them, and donkeys know where their master feeds them. But that is more than my people Israel know. They don't understand at all.

You have rejected the LORD, the Holy God of Israel, and have turned your backs on him.

From Isaiah 1:2–4

4 They refuse to return

The LORD says,
'When Israel was a child, I loved him and
    called him out of Egypt as my son.
But the more I called to him,
    the more he turned away from me.
Yet I was the one who taught Israel to
    walk.
I took my people up in my arms,
    but they did not acknowledge that I took
    care of them.
I drew them to me with affection and love.
I picked them up and held them to my
    cheek;
I bent down to them and fed them.
They refuse to return to me.'
From Hosea 11:1–5

5 Return to the LORD

Return to the LORD, and let this prayer be
your offering to him:

'Forgive all our sins and accept our prayer,
and we will praise you as we have
promised. We will never again say to our
idols that they are our God.'

The LORD says,
'I will bring my people back to me.
No longer am I angry with them.'
From Hosea 14:2–5

I will punish my people because they have sinned; they have abandoned me, have offered sacrifices to other gods, and have made idols and worshipped them. Go and tell them everything I command you to say. Do not be afraid of them.

They will not defeat you,
for I will be with you to protect you.
I, the LORD, have spoken.'
From Jeremiah 1:4–9,16–19

46 Proclaim what I command you

The LORD said to me, 'I chose you before I gave you life, and before you were born I selected you to be a prophet to the nations.'

I answered, 'Sovereign LORD, I don't know how to speak; I am too young.'

But the LORD said to me, 'Do not say that you are too young, but go to the people I send you to, and tell them everything I command you to say. Do not be afraid of them, for I will be with you to protect you. I, the LORD, have spoken!'

Then the LORD stretched out his hand, touched my lips, and said to me, 'Listen, I am giving you the words you must speak.

Come back to me!

Unfaithful Israel, come back to me.
I will not be angry with you for ever.
Only admit that you are guilty
and that you have rebelled against the LORD, your God.
Confess that you have not obeyed my commands.
From Jeremiah 3:12–13

18 You are this vineyard

Listen while I sing you this song,
  a song of my friend and his vineyard:

My friend had a vineyard on a very fertile hill.
He dug the soil and cleared it of stones;
  he planted the finest vines.
He waited for the grapes to ripen,
  but every grape was sour.

So now my friend says, 'This is what I am going
  to do to my vineyard;

I will take away the hedge round it,
  and let wild animals trample it down.
I will not prune the vines or hoe the ground;
  instead I will let briars and thorns cover it.

Israel is the vineyard of the LORD Almighty;
  the people of Judah are the vines he planted.
He expected them to do what was good, but instead
  they committed murder.
He expected them to do what was right, but their
  victims cried out for justice.

From Isaiah 5:1-7

10. God will come

The covenant with God was completely broken; the kingdom of Israel was in ruins. The people no longer lived in the promised land; they lived in captivity in a strange country.
Was all now lost? Had everything that God had begun now come to an end? It was at this point that the Israelites had a new discovery to make: God's dealings with them were not finished. He would make a new start.

The prophets announced that God himself would come and put things to rights. He would send a man, who would unite mankind to God afresh: the Messiah, also called the Christ. Through the Messiah a new world would begin, one in which God ruled: the kingdom of God.
Meanwhile the prophets continued to paint pictures of how things would be when God came to unite himself to mankind in a new way.

49 A new way

Comfort my people,
  comfort them!
Tell them they have suffered long enough
  and their sins are now forgiven.

Prepare in the wilderness a road for the LORD!
Clear the way in the desert for our God!
Fill every valley;
  level every mountain.

The hills will become a plain,
  and the rough country will be made smooth.

Then the glory of the LORD will be revealed,
  and all mankind will see it.

From Isaiah 40:1–5

A new covenant 50

The LORD says, 'The time is coming when I will make a new covenant with the people of Israel. It will not be like the old covenant that I made with their ancestors when I took them by the hand and led them out of Egypt. Although I was like a husband to them, they did not keep that covenant. The new covenant that I will make with the people of Israel will be this: I will put my law within them and write it on their hearts. I will be their God, and they will be my people. All will know me, from the least to the greatest. I will forgive their sins and I will no longer remember their wrongs.'

From Jeremiah 31:31–34

51 A new heart

I will give you a new heart and a new mind.

I will take away your stubborn heart of stone and give you an obedient heart.

I will put my spirit in you and I will see to it that you follow my laws and keep all the commands I have given you.

You will be my people,
and I will be your God.
From Ezekiel 36:26–28

A new shepherd 52

The Lord spoke to me.
'You are doomed, you shepherds of Israel!
You take care of yourselves,
but never tend the sheep.

You drink the milk,
wear clothes made from the wool,
and kill and eat the finest sheep.
But you never tend the sheep.

You have not taken care of the weak ones,
healed those that are sick,
bandaged those that are hurt,
brought back those that wandered off,
or looked for those that were lost.

Because the sheep had no shepherd,
they were scattered,
and wild animals killed and ate them.

I myself will look for my sheep
and take care of them.

I will look for those that are lost,
bring back those that wander off,
bandage those that are hurt,
and heal those that are sick.

I will give them a king
like my servant David
to be their one shepherd,
and he will take care of them.'
From Ezekiel 34:1–6,11,16,23

53 The Messiah

The spirit of the LORD will give him
   wisdom, and the knowledge and skill to
   rule his people.
He will know the LORD's will and honour
   him,
He will judge the poor fairly and
   defend the rights of the helpless.
From Isaiah 11:2–4

54 The people who walked in darkness
   have seen a great light.
They lived in a land of shadows,
   but now light is shining on them.
The boots of the invading army
   and all their bloodstained clothing
   will be destroyed by fire.
A child is born to us!
A son is given to us!
He will be called, 'Wonderful Counsellor,'
'Mighty God,' 'Eternal Father,'
'Prince of Peace.'
He will rule as King David's successor,
   basing his power on right and justice,
   from now until the end of time.
From Isaiah 9:2–7

How it will be in God's Kingdom 55

He will settle disputes among the nations,
   among the great powers near and far.
They will hammer their swords into ploughs
   and their spears into pruning-knives.
Nations will never again go to war,
   never prepare for battle again.
Everyone will live in peace
   among his own vineyards and fig-trees,
   and no one will make him afraid.
Micah 4:3–4

Wolves and sheep will live together in peace, **56**
   and leopards will lie down with young
   goats.
Calves and lion cubs will feed together,
   and little children will take care of them.
Cows and bears will eat together,
   and their calves and cubs will lie down in
   peace.
Lions will eat straw as cattle do.
Even a baby will not be harmed
   if it plays near a poisonous snake.
On Zion, God's sacred hill,
   there will be nothing harmful or evil.
The land will be as full of knowledge of
   the LORD as the seas are full of water.
Isaiah 11:6–9

Here on Mount Zion the LORD Almighty **57**
will prepare a banquet for all the nations
of the world.
The Sovereign LORD will destroy death
   for ever!
He will wipe away the tears from everyone's eyes.
From Isaiah 25:6–8

Encounters with God

God: holy and glorious
God: great and mighty
God: terrible and strong
God: merciful and kind
God: always and everywhere

God: you are with us
God: you have chosen us
God: you have set us free
God: you have guided us
God: you have given us this land

God: our Creator
God: our Lord
God: our King
God: our Deliverer
God: our Saviour

God: our shepherd
God: our rock
God: our stronghold
God: our light
God: our life

God: you are far away
God: you are near
God: you look upon us
God: you hear us
God: you forgive us

Praised be your name, O Lord!

From the prayers of Israel

II. God: in Jesus

We write to you about the Word of life, which has existed from the very beginning. We have heard it, and we have seen it with our eyes; yes, we have seen it, and our hands have touched it. What we have seen and heard we announce to you also, so that you will join with us in the fellowship that we have with the Father and with his Son Jesus Christ. We write this in order that our joy may be complete.

From 1 John 1:1–4

1. He is the Christ

You will give birth to a son

60

God sent the angel Gabriel to a town in Galilee named Nazareth. He had a message for a girl promised in marriage to a man named Joseph, who was a descendant of King David. The girl's name was Mary. The angel came to her and said, 'Peace be with you! The Lord is with you and has greatly blessed you! You will become pregnant and give birth to a son, and you will name him Jesus. He will be great and will be called the Son of the Most High God. The Lord God will make him a king, and his kingdom will never end!'

Mary said to the angel, 'I am a virgin. How, then, can this be?'

The angel answered, 'The Holy Spirit will come on you, and God's power will rest upon you. For this reason the holy child will be called the Son of God.'

'I am the Lord's servant,' said Mary; 'may it happen to me as you have said.' And the angel left her.

From Luke 1:26–38

Christ the Lord

61

At that time the Emperor Augustus ordered a census to be taken throughout the Roman Empire. Everyone went to register himself, each to his own town.

Joseph went from the town of Nazareth in Galilee to the town of Bethlehem in Judaea, the birthplace of King David. Joseph went there because he was a descendant of David. He went to register with Mary, who was promised in marriage to him. She was pregnant, and while they were in Bethlehem,

42

the time came for her to have her baby. She gave birth to her first son, wrapped him in strips of cloth and laid him in a manger – there was no room for them to stay in the inn.

There were some shepherds in that part of the country who were spending the night in the fields, taking care of their flocks. An angel of the Lord appeared to them, and the glory of the Lord shone over them. They were terribly afraid, but the angel said to them, 'Don't be afraid! I am here with good news for you. This very day in David's town your Saviour was born – Christ the Lord! And this is what will prove it to you: you will find a baby wrapped in strips of cloth and lying in a manger.'

Suddenly a great army of heaven's angels appeared with the angel, singing praises to God:
'Glory to God in the highest heaven, and peace on earth to those with whom he is pleased!'

When the angels went away from them back into heaven, the shepherds said to one another, 'Let's go to Bethlehem and see this thing that has happened, which the Lord has told us.'

So they hurried off and found Mary and Joseph and saw the baby lying in the manger. When the shepherds saw him, they told them what the angel had said about the child. All who heard it were amazed at what the shepherds said.

From Luke 2:1–18

62 They fell down before him

Jesus was born in the town of Bethlehem in Judaea. Soon afterwards, some men who studied the stars came from the east to Jerusalem and asked, 'Where is the baby born to be the king of the Jews? We saw his star when it came up in the east, and we have come to worship him.'

When King Herod heard about this, he was very upset. He called together all the chief priests and the teachers of the Law and asked them, 'Where will the Messiah be born?' 'In the town of Bethlehem in Judaea,' they answered.

So Herod called the visitors from the east to a secret meeting and found out from them the exact time the star had appeared. Then he sent them to Bethlehem with these instructions: 'Go and make a careful search for the child, and when you find him, let me know, so that I too may go and worship him.'

And so they left, and on their way they saw the same star they had seen in the east. It went ahead of them until it stopped over the place where the child was. They went into the house, and when they saw the child with his mother Mary, they knelt down and worshipped him. They brought out their gifts of gold, frankincense, and myrrh, and presented them to him.

Then they returned to their country by another road, since God had warned them in a dream not to go back to Herod.

From Matthew 2:1–12

2. We have found him

63 Get the road ready for the Lord

It was the fifteenth year of the rule of the Emperor Tiberius; Pontius Pilate was governor of Judaea. At that time the word of God came to John son of Zechariah in the desert. So John went throughout the whole territory of the River Jordan, preaching, 'Turn away from your sins and be baptized, and God will forgive your sins.' As it is written in the book of the prophet Isaiah:

Someone is shouting in the desert:
'Get the road ready for the Lord;
   make a straight path for him to travel!
Every valley must be filled up
   every hill and mountain levelled off.
The winding roads must be made straight,
   and the rough paths made smooth.
All mankind will see God's salvation!'

Crowds of people came out to John to be baptized by him. 'You snakes!' he said to them. 'Do those things that will show that you have turned from your sins. And don't start saying among yourselves that Abraham is your ancestor. I tell you that God can take these stones and make descendants for Abraham! The axe is ready to cut down the trees at the roots; every tree that does not bear good fruit will be cut down and thrown in the fire.'

From Luke 3:1–9

He comes after me 64

The Jewish authorities in Jerusalem sent some priests and Levites to John, to ask him, 'Who are you?' John did not refuse to answer, but spoke out openly and clearly, saying: 'I am not the Messiah.'

'Then tell us who you are,' they said. 'We have to take an answer back to those who sent us. What do you say about yourself?'

John answered, 'I baptize with water, but among you stands the one you do not know. He is coming after me, but I am not good enough even to untie his sandals.'

From John 1:19–27

65 We have found the Messiah

The next day John was standing there again with two of his disciples, when he saw Jesus walking by. 'There is the Lamb of God!' he said.

The two disciples heard him say this and went with Jesus. Jesus turned, saw them following him, and asked, 'What are you looking for?'

They answered, 'Where do you live, Rabbi?' (This word means 'Teacher'.)

'Come and see,' he answered. So they went with him and saw where he lived, and spent the rest of that day with him.

From John 1:35–39

66

One of them was Andrew, Simon Peter's brother. At once he found his brother Simon and told him, 'We have found the Messiah.' (This word means 'Christ'.)

John 1:40–41

Out of Nazareth 67

The next day Jesus decided to go to Galilee. He found Philip and said to him, 'Come with me!' Philip found Nathanael and told him, 'We have found the one whom Moses wrote about in the book of the Law and whom the prophets also wrote about. he is Jesus son of Joseph, from Nazareth.'

'Can anything good come from Nazareth?' Nathanael asked.

'Come and see,' answered Philip.

When Jesus saw Nathanael coming to him, he said about him, 'Here is a real Israelite; there is nothing false in him!'

Nathanael asked him, 'How do you know me?' Jesus answered, 'I saw you when you were under the fig-tree before Philip called you.'

'Teacher,' answered Nathanael, 'you are the Son of God! You are the King of Israel!'

Jesus said, 'Do you believe just because I told you I saw you when you were under the fig-tree? You will see much greater things than this!'

John 1:43–50

68 From now on you will be catching men

One day Jesus was standing on the shore of Lake Gennesaret while the people pushed their way up to him to listen to the word of God. He saw two boats pulled up on the beach; the fishermen had left them and were washing the nets. Jesus got into one of the boats – it belonged to Simon – and asked him to push off a little from the shore. Jesus sat in the boat and taught the crowd.

When he finished speaking, he said to Simon, 'Push the boat out further to the deep water, and you and your partners let down your nets for a catch.' 'Master,' Simon answered, 'we worked hard all night long and caught nothing. But if you say so, I will let down the nets.' They let them down and caught such a large number of fish that the nets were about to break. So they motioned to their partners in the other boat to come and help them. They came and filled both boats so full of fish that the boats were about to sink. When Simon Peter saw what had happened, he fell on his knees before Jesus and said, 'Go away from me, Lord! I am a sinful man!'

Jesus said to Simon, 'Don't be afraid; from now on you will be catching men.'

They pulled the boats up on the beach, left everything, and followed Jesus. From Luke 5:1–11

Follow me 69

After this, Jesus went out and saw a tax collector named Levi, sitting in his office. Jesus said to him, 'Follow me.' Levi got up, left everything, and followed him.

Then Levi had a big feast in his house for Jesus, and among the guests was a large number of tax collectors and other people. Some Pharisees and some teachers of the Law who belonged to their group complained to Jesus' disciples. 'Why do you eat and drink with tax collectors and other outcasts?' they asked.

Jesus answered them, 'People who are well do not need a doctor, but only those who are sick. I have not come to call respectable people to repent, but outcasts.' Luke 5:27–32

3. They were astonished at his teaching

70 The Kingdom of God

Jesus went to Galilee and preached the Good News from God. 'The right time has come,' he said, 'and the Kingdom of God is near! Turn away from your sins and believe the Good News!'

Mark 1:14–15

71 They were amazed

Jesus and his disciples came to the town of Capernaum, and on the next Sabbath Jesus went to the synagogue and began to teach. The people who heard him were amazed at the way he taught, for he wasn't like the teachers of the Law; instead, he taught with authority.

Mark 1:21–22

72 They took offence at him

Mark's account:

Jesus left that place and went back to his home town, followed by his disciples. On the Sabbath he began to teach in the synagogue. Many people were there; and when they heard him, they were all amazed. 'Where did he get all this?' they asked. 'What wisdom is this that has been given him? How does he perform miracles? Isn't he the carpenter, the son of Mary?' And so they rejected him.

Jesus said to them, 'A prophet is respected everywhere except in his own home town.'

He was greatly surprised, because the people did not have faith.

From Mark 6:1–6

73

Luke's account:

Then Jesus went to Nazareth, where he had been brought up, and on the Sabbath he went as usual to the synagogue. He stood up to read the Scriptures and was handed the book of the prophet Isaiah. He unrolled the scroll and found the place where it is written,

'The Spirit of the Lord is upon me,
    because he has chosen me to bring good news to the poor.'

Jesus rolled up the scroll, gave it back to the attendant, and sat down. All the people in the synagogue had their eyes fixed on him, as he said to them, 'This passage of scripture has come true today, as you heard it being read.'

They were all well impressed with him and marvelled at the eloquent words that he spoke. They said, 'Isn't he the son of Joseph?'

He said to them, 'I am sure that you will quote this proverb to me, "Doctor, heal yourself." You will also tell me to do here in my home town the same things you heard were done in Capernaum. I tell you this,' Jesus added, 'a prophet is never welcomed in his home town.'

When the people in the synagogue heard this, they were filled with anger. They rose up, dragged Jesus out of the town, and took him to the top of the hill on which their town was built. They meant to throw him over the cliff, but he walked through the middle of the crowd and went his way.

From Luke 4:16–24,28–30

74 Good News

Jesus went all over Galilee, teaching in the synagogues, preaching the Good News about the Kingdom, and healing people who had all kinds of disease and sickness. The news about him spread through the whole country. Large crowds followed him from Galilee and the land on the other side of the Jordan.

Jesus saw the crowds and went up a hill, where he sat down. His disciples gathered round him, and he began to teach them:

'Happy are those who know they are spiritually poor;
the Kingdom of heaven belongs to them!
'Happy are those who mourn;
God will comfort them!

'Happy are those who are humble;
they will receive what God has promised!
'Happy are those whose greatest desire is to do what God requires;
God will satisfy them fully!
'Happy are those who are merciful to others;
God will be merciful to them!
'Happy are the pure in heart;
they will see God!
'Happy are those who work for peace;
God will call them his children!
'Happy are those who are persecuted because they do what God requires; the Kingdom of heaven belongs to them!'

From Matthew 4:23 – 5:10

49

75 Who belongs to Jesus?

Jesus' mother and brothers arrived. They stood outside and sent in a message, asking for him. A crowd was sitting round Jesus, and they said to him, 'Look, your mother and your brothers and sisters are outside, and they want you.'
Jesus answered, 'Who is my mother? Who are my brothers? Whoever does what God wants him to do is my brother, my sister, my mother.'
From Mark 3:31-35

76 Who is the greatest?

They came to Capernaum, and after going indoors Jesus asked his disciples, 'What were you arguing about on the road?'
But they would not answer him, because on the road they had been arguing among themselves about who was the greatest. Jesus sat down, called the twelve disciples, and said to them, 'Whoever wants to be first must place himself last of all and be the servant of all.' Then he took a child and made him stand in front of them. He put his arms round him and said to them, 'Whoever welcomes in my name one of these children, welcomes me; and whoever welcomes me, welcomes not only me but also the one who sent me.'
Mark 9:33-37

Who gave more? 77

As Jesus sat near the temple treasury, he watched the people as they dropped in their money. Many rich men dropped in a lot of money; then a poor widow came along and dropped in two little copper coins, worth about a penny. He called his disciples together and said to them, 'I tell you that this poor widow put more in the offering box than all the others. For the others put in what they had to spare of their riches; but she, poor as she is, put in all she had – she gave all she had to live on.'
Mark 12:41-44

Who is the greatest? 78

An argument broke out among the disciples as to which one of them should be thought of as the greatest. Jesus said to them, 'The kings of the pagans have power over their people, and the rulers are called "Friends of the People." But this is not the way it is with you; rather, the greatest one among you must be like the youngest, and the leader must be like the servant. Who is greater, the one who sits down to eat or the one who serves him? The one who sits down, of course. But I am among you as one who serves.'
Luke 22:24-27

79 To whom does the Kingdom of God belong?

Some people brought children to Jesus for him to place his hands on them, but the disciples scolded the people.

When Jesus noticed this, he was angry and said to his disciples, 'Let the children come to me, and do not stop them, because the Kingdom of God belongs to such as these. I assure you that whoever does not receive the Kingdom of God like a child will never enter it.' Then he took the children in his arms, placed his hands on each of them, and blessed them.

Mark 10:13–16

When will the Kingdom of God come? 80

Some Pharisees asked Jesus when the Kingdom of God would come. His answer was, 'The Kingdom of God does not come in such a way as to be seen. No one will say, "Look, here it is!" or, "There it is!"; because the Kingdom of God is among you.'

Luke 17:20–21

A teacher of the Law came up and tried to trap Jesus. 'Teacher,' he asked, 'what must I do to receive eternal life?'

Jesus answered him, 'What do the Scriptures say? How do you interpret them?'

The man answered, '"Love the Lord your God with all your heart, with all your soul, with all your strength, and with all your mind"; and "Love your neighbour as you love yourself."'

'You are right,' Jesus replied; 'do this and you will live.'

Luke 10:25–28

But the teacher of the Law wanted to justify himself, so he asked Jesus, 'Who is my neighbour?'

Jesus answered, 'There was once a man who was going down from Jerusalem to Jericho when robbers attacked him, stripped him, and beat him up, leaving him half dead. It so happened that a priest was going down that road; but when he saw the man, he walked on by, on the other side. In the same way a Levite also came along, went over and looked at the man, and then walked on by, on the other side. But a Samaritan who was travelling that way came upon the man, and when he saw him, his heart was filled with pity. He went over to him, poured oil and wine on his wounds and bandaged them; then he put the man on his own animal and took him to an inn, where he took care of him. The next day he took out two silver coins and gave them to the innkeeper. "Take care of him," he told the innkeeper, "and when I come back this way, I will pay you whatever else you spend on him."'

And Jesus concluded, 'In your opinion, which one of these three acted like a neighbour towards the man attacked by the robbers?'

The teacher of the Law answered, 'The one who was kind to him.'

Jesus replied, 'You go, then, and do the same.'

Luke 10:29–37

3 Who bears good fruit?

Jesus went to the lake-side, where he sat down to teach. The crowd that gathered round him was so large that he got into a boat and sat in it, while the crowds stood on the shore. He used parables to tell them many things.

'Once there was a man who went out to sow corn. As he scattered the seed in the field, some of it fell along the path, and the birds came and ate it up. Some of it fell on rocky ground, where there was little soil. The seeds soon sprouted, because the soil wasn't deep. But when the sun came up, it burnt the young plants; and because the roots had not grown deep enough, the plants soon dried up. Some of the seed fell among thorn bushes, which grew up and choked the plants. But some seeds fell in good soil, and the plants produced corn; some produced a hundred gains, others sixty, and others thirty.'

'Listen, then, and learn what the parable of the sower means. Those who hear the message about the Kingdom but do not understand it are like the seeds that fell along the path. The Evil One comes and snatches away what was sown in them. The seeds that fell on rocky ground stand for those who receive the message gladly as soon as they hear it. But it does not sink deep into them, and they don't last long. The seeds that fell among thorn bushes stand for those who hear the message; but the worries about this life and the love for riches choke the message, and they don't bear fruit. And the seeds sown in the good soil stand for those who hear the message and understand it: they bear fruit, some as much as a hundred, others sixty, and others thirty.'

From Matthew 13:1–9,18–23

What is the Kingdom of heaven like? 8▪

The Kingdom of heaven is like this. A man happens to find a treasure hidden in a field. He covers it up again, and is so happy that he goes and sells everything he has, and then goes back and buys that field.
Matthew 13:44

Also, the Kingdom of heaven is like this. A man 8**5** is looking for fine pearls, and when he finds one that is unusually fine, he goes and sells everything he has, and buys that pearl.
Matthew 13:45

The Kingdom of heaven is like this. A woman 8**6** takes some yeast and mixes it with forty litres of flour until the whole batch of dough rises.
Matthew 13:33

The Kingdom of
heaven is like this.
A man takes a
mustard seed and
sows it in his field.
It is the smallest of
all seeds, but when
it grows up, it is the
biggest of all plants.
It becomes a tree,
so that birds come
and make their nests
in its branches.

Matthew 13: 31–32

4. He can heal anyone

88 Be opened

Some people brought him a man who was deaf
and could hardly speak, and they begged Jesus
to place his hands on him. So Jesus took him
off alone, away from the crowd, put his fingers
in the man's ears, spat, and touched the man's
tongue. Then Jesus looked up to heaven, gave a
deep groan, and said to the man, '*Ephphatha*,' which
means, 'Open up!'

At once the man was able to hear, his speech
impediment was removed, and he began to talk
without any trouble.

And all who heard were completely amazed. 'How
well he does everything!' they exclaimed. 'He even
causes the deaf to hear and the dumb to speak!'

From Mark 7:32–37

89 Sir, if you want to

A man suffering from a dreaded skin-disease came
to him, knelt down before him, and said, 'Sir,
if you want to, you can make me clean.' Jesus
stretched out his hand and touched him. 'I do
want to,' he answered. 'Be clean!' At once the
man was healed of his disease.

Matthew 8:2–3

90 Take pity on me

They came to Jericho, and as Jesus was leaving
with his disciples and a large crowd, a blind beggar
named Bartimaeus was sitting by the road. When
he heard that it was Jesus of Nazareth, he began
to shout, 'Jesus! Son of David! Take pity on me!'
Many of the people scolded him and told him
to be quiet. But he shouted even more loudly,
'Son of David, take pity on me!'

Jesus stopped and said, 'Call him.'

So they called the blind man. 'Cheer up!' they
said. 'Get up, he is calling you.'

He threw off his cloak, jumped up, and came
to Jesus. 'What do you want me to do for you?'
Jesus asked him.

'Teacher,' the blind man answered, 'I want to
see again.'

'Go,' Jesus told him, 'your faith has made you
well.'

At once he was able to see and followed Jesus
on the road.

Mark 10:46–52

91 Just give the order

Jesus went to Capernaum. A Roman officer there had a servant who was sick and about to die. When the officer heard about Jesus, he sent some Jewish elders to ask him to come and heal his servant. They came to Jesus and begged him earnestly, 'This man really deserves your help. He loves our people and he himself built a synagogue for us.'
So Jesus went with them. He was not far from the house when the officer sent friends to tell him, 'Sir, don't trouble yourself. I do not deserve to have you come into my house. Just give the order, and my servant will get well.'
Jesus was surprised when he heard this; he turned round and said to the crowd following him, 'I tell you, I have never found faith like this, not even in Israel!' The messengers went back to the officer's house and found his servant well.

From Luke 7:1–10

92 His heart was filled with pity

Soon afterwards Jesus went to a town called Nain, accompanied by his disciples and a large crowd. Just as he arrived at the gate of the town, a funeral procession was coming out. The dead man was the only son of a woman who was a widow, and a large crowd from the town was with her. When the Lord saw her, his heart was filled with pity for her, and he said to her, 'Don't cry.' Then he walked over and touched the coffin, and the men carrying it stopped. Jesus said, 'Young man! Get up, I tell you!' The dead man sat up and began to talk, and Jesus gave him back to his mother. They all were filled with fear and praised God. 'A great prophet has appeared among us!' they said; 'God has come to save his people!'
Luke 7:11–16

Who can forgive sins? 93

Jesus went to Capernaum. So many people came together that there was no room left, not even out in front of the door. Jesus was preaching the message to them when four men arrived, carrying a paralysed man to Jesus. Because of the crowd, however, they could not get the man to him. So they made a hole in the roof right above the place where Jesus was. When they had made an opening, they let the man down, lying on his mat. Seeing how much faith they had, Jesus said to the paralysed man, 'My son, your sins are forgiven.'
Some teachers of the Law who were sitting there thought to themselves, 'How does he dare to talk like this? This is blasphemy! God is the only one who can forgive sins!'
At once Jesus knew what they were thinking, so he said to them, 'Why do you think such things? Is it easier to say to this paralysed man, "Your sins are forgiven", or to say, "Get up, pick up your mat, and walk"? I will prove to you, then, that the Son of Man has authority on earth to forgive sins.' So he said to the paralysed man, 'I tell you, get up, pick up your mat, and go home!'
While they all watched, the man got up, picked up his mat, and hurried away. They were all completely amazed and praised God, saying, 'We have never seen anything like this!'
Mark 2:1–12

94 Are you the one who is to come?

When John's disciples told him about all these things, he called two of them and sent them to the Lord to ask him, 'Are you the one John said was going to come, or should we expect someone else?'

When they came to Jesus, they said, 'John the Baptist sent us to ask if you are the one he said was going to come, or should we expect someone else?'

At that very time Jesus cured many people of their sicknesses, diseases, and evil spirits, and gave sight to many blind people. He answered John's messengers, 'Go back and tell John what you have seen and heard:

The blind can see,
the lame can walk,
those who suffer from dreaded skin-
diseases are made clean,
the deaf can hear,
the dead are raised to life,
and the Good News is preached to the
poor.'

Luke 7:18–22

5. Who is this man?

95 Because he called God his father

Jesus went to Jerusalem for a religious festival. A man was there who had been ill for thirty-eight years.

Jesus said to him, 'Get up, pick up your mat, and walk.' Immediately the man got well; he picked up his mat and started walking.

The day this happened was a Sabbath, so the Jewish authorities told the man who had been healed, 'This is a Sabbath, and it is against our Law for you to carry your mat.'

He answered, 'The man who made me well told me to pick up my mat and walk.' They asked him, 'Who is the man who told you to do this?' But the man who had been healed did not know who Jesus was.

Afterwards, Jesus found him in the Temple. Then the man left and told the Jewish authorities that it was Jesus who had healed him. So they began to persecute Jesus, because he had done this healing on a Sabbath. Jesus answered them, 'My Father is always working, and I too must work.'

This saying made the Jewish authorities all the more determined to kill him; not only had he broken the Sabbath law, but he had said that God was his own Father and in this way had made himself equal with God.   From John 5:1–18

96 The Prophet?

Jesus went across Lake Galilee. A large crowd followed him. Jesus went up a hill and sat down with his disciples. He asked Philip, 'Where can we buy enough food to feed all these people?' (He said this to test Philip; actually he already knew what he would do.)

Philip answered, 'For everyone to have even a little, it would take more than two hundred silver coins to buy enough bread.'

Another of his disciples, Andrew, said, 'There is a boy here who has five loaves of barley bread and two fish. But they will certainly not be enough for all these people.' 'Make the people sit down,' Jesus told them. (There was a lot of grass there.) So all the people sat down; there were about five thousand men. Jesus took the bread, gave thanks to God, and distributed it to the people who were sitting there. He did the same with the fish, and they all had as much as they wanted. When they were all full, he said to his disciples, 'Gather the pieces left over; let us not waste any.' So they gathered them all up and filled twelve baskets with the pieces left over from the five barley loaves which the people had eaten.

Seeing this miracle that Jesus had performed, the people there said, 'Surely this is the Prophet who was to come into the world!' Jesus knew that they were about to come and seize him in order to make him king by force; so he went off again to the hills by himself.   From John 6:1–15

Whoever eats me   97

Next day the crowd which had stayed on the other side of the lake saw that Jesus was not there, so they went to Capernaum, looking for him.

Jesus said, 'You are looking for me because you ate the bread and had all you wanted, not because you understood my miracles. Do not work for food that goes bad; instead, work for the food that lasts for eternal life. For the bread that God gives is he who comes down from heaven. I am the bread of life.'

The people started grumbling about him, because he said, 'I am the bread that came down from heaven.' So they said, 'This man is Jesus son of Joseph, isn't he? We know his father and mother.' Jesus answered, 'Stop grumbling among yourselves. I am the living bread that came down from heaven. If anyone eats this bread, he will live for ever. The bread that I will give him is my flesh, which I give so that the world may live.'

This started an angry argument among them. 'How can this man give us his flesh to eat?' they asked. Jesus said to them, 'Whoever eats my flesh and drinks my blood lives in me, and I live in him. The living Father sent me, and because of him I live also. In the same way whoever eats me will live because of me.'

Many of his followers heard this and said, 'This teaching is too hard. Who can listen to it?' Because of this, many turned back and would not go with him any more. So he asked the twelve disciples, 'And you – would you also like to leave?'

Simon Peter answered him, 'Lord, to whom would we go? You have the words that give eternal life. And now we believe and know that you are the Holy One who has come from God.'

From John 6:22–69

98 They quarrelled about him

After his brothers had gone to the festival, Jesus also went. The Jewish authorities were looking for him at the festival. 'Where is he?' they asked. There was much whispering about him in the crowd. 'He is a good man,' some people said. 'No,' others said, 'he is misleading the people.'
From John 7:10–12

99 How does this man know so much?

The festival was nearly half over when Jesus went to the Temple and began teaching. The Jewish authorities were greatly surprised and said, 'How does this man know so much when he has never had any training?' Jesus answered, 'What I teach is not my own teaching, but it comes from God, who sent me.'
John 7:14–16

100 Is he the Messiah?

Some of the people in the crowd heard him say this and said, 'This man is really the Prophet!' Others said, 'He is the Messiah!'
But others said, 'The Messiah will not come from Galilee! The scripture says that the Messiah will be a descendant of King David and will be born in Bethlehem, the town where David lived.' So there was a division in the crowd because of Jesus. Some wanted to seize him, but no one laid a hand on him.
When the guards went back, the chief priests and Pharisees asked them, 'Why did you not bring him?' The guards answered, 'Nobody has ever talked like this man!'
'Did he fool you, too?' the Pharisees asked them.
John 7:40–47

Who are you? 10

It was winter, and the Festival of the Dedication of the Temple was being celebrated in Jerusalem. Jesus was walking in the Temple, when the people gathered round him and asked, 'How long are you going to keep us in suspense? Tell us the plain truth: are you the Messiah?'

Jesus answered,
'I have already told you,
but you would not believe me.
The Father and I are one.'

Then the people picked up stones to throw at him.

Jesus said to them,
'I have done many good deeds in your presence which the Father gave me to do;
for which one of these do you want to stone me?'

They replied, 'We do not want to stone you because of any good deeds, but because of your blasphemy! You are only a man, but you are trying to make yourself God!'

Jesus answered,
'Do not believe me, then, but you should at least believe my deeds, in order that you may know once and for all that the Father is in me and that I am in the Father.'   From John 10:22–39

6. My life – for you

102 God bless the king!

Jesus went on to Jerusalem. He sent two disciples ahead with these instructions: 'Go to the village there ahead of you; as you go in, you will find a colt tied up that has never been ridden. Untie it and bring it here. If someone asks you why you are untying it, tell him that the Master needs it.' They went on their way and took the colt to Jesus. Then they threw their cloaks over the animal and helped Jesus get on. As he rode on, people spread their cloaks on the road.

When he came near Jerusalem, the large crowd of his disciples began to thank God and praise him in loud voices for all the great things that they had seen.

'God bless the king
who comes in
the name of
the Lord!
Peace in heaven
and glory to God!'
From Luke 19:28–38

They tried to find a way

The time was near for the Passover. The chief priests and the teachers of the Law were afraid of the people, and so they were trying to find a way of putting Jesus to death secretly.

Then Satan entered Judas, called Iscariot, who was one of the twelve disciples. So Judas went off and spoke with the chief priests and the officers of the temple guard about how he could betray Jesus to them. They were pleased and offered to pay him money. Judas agreed to it and started looking for a good chance to hand Jesus over to them without the people knowing about it.

From Luke 22:1–6

04 My body – for you

The day came when the lambs for the Passover meal were to be killed. Jesus sent off Peter and John with these instructions: 'Go and get the Passover meal ready for us to eat.' 'Where do you want us to get it ready?' they asked him. He answered, 'As you go into the city, a man carrying a jar of water will meet you. Follow him into the house that he enters. He will show you a large furnished room upstairs, where you will get everything ready.'

They went off and found everything just as Jesus had told them, and they prepared the passover meal.

When the hour came, Jesus took his place at the table with the apostles. He said to them, 'I have wanted so much to eat this Passover meal with you before I suffer!'

Then he took a piece of bread, gave thanks to God, broke it, and gave it to them, saying, 'This is my body, which is given for you. Do this in memory of me.' In the same way, he gave them the cup after the supper, saying, 'This cup is God's new covenant sealed with my blood, which is poured out for you.'

From Luke 22:7–20

Betrayed!

Jesus was still speaking when a crowd arrived, led by Judas. He came up to Jesus to kiss him. But Jesus said, 'Judas, is it with a kiss that you betray the Son of Man?'

When the disciples saw what was going to happen, they asked, 'Shall we use our swords, Lord?' And one of them struck the High Priest's slave and cut off his right ear.

But Jesus said, 'Enough of this!' He touched the man's ear and healed him.

Then Jesus said to the chief priests and the officers of the temple guard, 'Did you have to come with swords and clubs, as though I were an outlaw? I was with you in the Temple every day, and you did not try to arrest me. But this is your hour to act, when the power of darkness rules.'

From Luke 22:47–53

105 In great anguish

Jesus went to the Mount of Olives; and the disciples went with him. When he arrived at the place, he went off from them and knelt down and prayed. 'Father,' he said, 'if you will, take this cup of suffering away from me. Not my will, however, but your will be done.' An angel from heaven appeared to him and strengthened him. In great anguish he prayed even more fervently; his sweat was like drops of blood falling to the ground. Rising from his prayer, he went back to the disciples and found them asleep. He said to them, 'Why are you sleeping? Get up and pray that you will not fall into temptation.'   From Luke 22:39–46

107 Beaten

They arrested Jesus and took him away into the house of the High Priest. The men who were guarding Jesus mocked him and beat him. They blindfolded him and asked him, 'Who hit you? Guess!'
When day came, the elders, the chief priests, and the teachers of the Law met together, and Jesus was brought before the Council. 'Tell us,' they said, 'are you the Messiah?'
He answered, 'From now on the Son of Man will be seated on the right of Almighty God.'
They all said, 'Are you, then, the Son of God?'
He answered them, 'You say that I am.'
And they said, 'We don't need any witnesses! We ourselves have heard what he said!'

From Luke 22:54,63–71

108 Accused

The whole group rose up and took Jesus before Pilate, where they began to accuse him: 'We caught this man misleading our people, claiming that he is the Messiah, a king.'
Pilate asked him, 'Are you the king of the Jews?'
'So you say,' answered Jesus.
Then Pilate said to the chief priests and the crowds, 'I find no reason to condemn this man.'
When Pilate learnt that Jesus was from the region ruled by Herod, he sent him to Herod, who was also in Jerusalem at that time. Herod was very pleased when he saw Jesus, because he had heard about him and was hoping to see Jesus perform some miracle. So Herod asked Jesus many questions, but Jesus made no answer. Herod and his soldiers mocked Jesus; then they put a fine robe on him and sent him back to Pilate.

From Luke 23:1–11

Condemned 109

Pilate said, 'There is nothing this man has done to deserve death. So I will have him whipped and let him go.' But they shouted back, 'Crucify him! Crucify him!' Pilate said to them, 'But what crime has he committed? I cannot find he has done anything to deserve death!'
But they kept on shouting that Jesus should be crucified, and finally their shouting succeeded. So Pilate passed the sentence on Jesus that they were asking for.   From Luke 23:13–16,21–24

0 Dead

The soldiers led Jesus away. When they came to the place called 'The Skull,' they crucified Jesus there, and the two criminals. Jesus said, 'Forgive them, Father! They don't know what they are doing.'

They divided his clothes among themselves by throwing dice. The people stood there watching while the Jewish leaders jeered at him: 'He saved others; let him save himself if he is the Messiah whom God has chosen!' The soldiers also mocked him: they came up to him and offered him cheap wine, and said, 'Save yourself if you are the king of the Jews!'

Above him were written these words: 'This is the King of the Jews.'

It was about twelve o'clock when the sun stopped shining and darkness covered the whole country until three o'clock. Jesus cried out in a loud voice, 'Father! In your hands I place my spirit!' He said this and died.

From Luke 23:26,32–38,44–46

1 Buried

There was a man named Joseph from Arimathea, a town in Judaea. He was a good and honourable man, who was waiting for the coming of the Kingdom of God. Although he was a member of the Council, he had not agreed with their decision and action. He went into the presence of Pilate and asked for the body of Jesus. Then he took the body down, wrapped it in a linen sheet, and placed it in a tomb which had been dug out of solid rock and which had never been used. It was Friday, and the Sabbath was about to begin.

Luke 23:50–54

7. He lives

The guarantee

He has been raised!

And now I want to remind you, my brothers, of the Good News which I preached to you, that Christ died for our sins; that he was buried and that he was raised to life three days later; that he appeared to Peter and then to all twelve apostles. Then he appeared to more than five hundred of his followers at once. Then he appeared to James, and afterwards to all the apostles. Last of all he appeared to me.

Christ has been raised from death, as the guarantee that those who sleep in death will also be raised.

From a letter from the apostle Paul
1 Corinthians 15:1–8,20

After the Sabbath was over, Mary Magdalene, Mary the mother of James, and Salome bought spices to go and anoint the body of Jesus. Very early on Sunday morning, at sunrise, they went to the tomb. On the way they said to one another, 'Who will roll away the stone for us from the entrance to the tomb?' (It was a very large stone.) Then they looked up and saw that the stone had already been rolled back. So they entered the tomb, where they saw a young man sitting on the right, wearing a white robe – and they were alarmed. 'Don't be alarmed,' he said. 'I know you are looking for Jesus of Nazareth, who was crucified. He is not here – he has been raised! Look, here is the place where they put him. Now go and give this message to his disciples, including Peter: "He is going to Galilee ahead of you; there you will see him, just as he told you."'

So they went out and ran from the tomb, distressed and terrified. They said nothing to anyone, because they were afraid.

Mark 16:1–8

114 Then their eyes were opened

On that same day two of Jesus' followers were going to a village named Emmaus, and they were talking to each other about all the things that had happened. As they talked and discussed, Jesus himself drew near and walked along with them; they saw him, but somehow did not recognize him. Jesus said to them, 'What are you talking about to each other, as you walk along?'

They stood still, with sad faces. One of them, named Cleopas, asked him, 'Are you the only visitor in Jerusalem who doesn't know the things that have been happening there these last few days?'

'What things?' he asked.

'The things that happened to Jesus of Nazareth,' they answered. 'This man was a prophet and was powerful in everything he said and did. Our chief priests and rulers handed him over to be sentenced to death, and he was crucified. And we had hoped that he would be the one who was going to set Israel free! Besides all that, this is now the third day since it happened. Some of the women of our group surprised us; they went at dawn to the tomb, but could not find his body. They came back saying they had seen a vision of angels who told them that he is alive. Some of our group went to the tomb and found it exactly as the women had said, but they did not see him.'

Then Jesus said to them, 'How slow you are to believe everything the prophets said! Was it not necessary for the Messiah to suffer these things and then to enter his glory?'

As they came near the village to which they were going, Jesus acted as if he were going farther; but they held him back, saying, 'Stay with us; the day is almost over and it is getting dark.' So he went in to stay with them. He sat down

to eat with them, took the bread, and said the blessing; then he broke the bread and gave it to them. Then their eyes were opened and they recognized him, but he disappeared from their sight.

From Luke 24:13–31

Feel me!   115

While the two were telling the others of all this, suddenly the Lord himself stood among them.

They were terrified, thinking that they were seeing a ghost. But he said to them, 'Why are you alarmed? Look at my hands and my feet, and see that it is I myself. Feel me, and you will know, for a ghost doesn't have flesh and bones, as you can see I have.'

He said this and showed them his hands and his feet. They still could not believe, they were so full of joy and wonder; so he asked them, 'Have you anything here to eat?' They gave him a piece of cooked fish, which he took and ate in their presence.

From Luke 24:36–43

My Lord and my God!   **116**

One of the twelve disciples Thomas (called the Twin), was not with them when Jesus came. So the other disciples told him, 'We have seen the Lord!'

Thomas said to them, 'Unless I see the scars of the nails in his hands and put my finger on those scars and my hand in his side, I will not believe.' A week later the disciples were together again indoors, and Thomas was with them. The doors were locked, but Jesus came and stood among them and said, 'Peace be with you.' Then he said to Thomas, 'Put your finger here, and look at my hands; then stretch out your hand and put it in my side. Stop your doubting, and believe!' Thomas answered him, 'My Lord and my God!'

Jesus said to him, 'Do you believe because you see me? How happy are those who believe without seeing me!'

John 20:24–29

Be glad   **117**

Peace is what I leave with you.
Do not be worried and upset.
I am leaving,
but I will come back to you.
If you loved me,
you would be glad that I am going to the Father;
for he is greater than I.
From John 14:27–28

118 Taken up to heaven

'When the Holy Spirit comes upon you, you will be filled with power, and you will be witnesses for me to the ends of the earth.'
After saying this, Jesus was taken up to heaven as they watched him, and a cloud hid him from their sight.
They still had their eyes fixed on the sky as he went away, when two men dressed in white suddenly stood beside them and said, 'Galileans, why are you standing there looking up at the sky? This Jesus, who was taken from you into heaven, will come back in the same way that you saw him go to heaven.'
From Acts 1:8–11

119 God has made him Lord

Let us give thanks to the God and Father of our Lord Jesus Christ! He raised Christ from death and seated him at his right side in the heavenly world. Christ rules there above all. God put all things under Christ's feet as supreme Lord over all things.
From Ephesians 1:3,20–22

120 Now, there are many other things that Jesus did. If they were all written down one by one, I suppose that the whole world could not hold the books that would be written.
John 21:25

Jesus Christ is Lord

He always had the nature of God,
but he did not think that by force
he should try to become equal with God.

Instead of this, he gave up all he had,
and took the nature of a servant.

He became like man.
He was humble and walked the path of
   obedience
all the way to death—
his death on the cross.

For this reason God raised him to the
   highest place above
and gave him the name that is greater
   than any other name.

And so, in honour of the name of Jesus
all beings in heaven, on earth, and in
the world below
will fall on their knees,
and all will openly proclaim that

Jesus Christ is Lord.

From Philippians 2:6–11

III.
God:
in the
midst
of us

They were filled with the Holy Spirit **122**

When the day of Pentecost came, all the believers were gathered together in one place. Suddenly there was a noise from the sky which sounded like a strong wind blowing, and it filled the whole house where they were sitting. Then they saw what looked like tongues of fire which spread out and touched each person there. They were filled with the Holy Spirit.

Acts 2:1–4

What does this mean?

When they heard this noise, a large crowd gathered. They were all excited, because each one of them heard the believers speaking in his own language. Amazed and confused, they kept asking each other, 'What does this mean?'
But others made fun of the believers, saying, 'These people are drunk!'
Then Peter stood up with the other eleven apostles and began to speak to the crowd: 'Jesus of Nazareth was a man whose divine authority was clearly proven to you by all the miracles and wonders which God performed through him. You yourselves know this, for it happened here among you, and you killed him by letting sinful men crucify him.
'God has raised this very Jesus from death, and we are all witnesses to this fact. What you now see and hear is his gift that he has poured out on us.'
From Acts 2:6–33

What shall we do?

When the people heard this, they were deeply troubled and said to Peter and the other apostles, 'What shall we do, brothers?'
Peter said to them, 'Each one of you must turn away from his sins and be baptized in the name of Jesus Christ, so that your sins will be forgiven; and you will receive God's gift, the Holy Spirit.'
Many of them believed his message and were baptized, and about three thousand people were added to the group that day.
They spent their time in learning from the apostles, taking part in the fellowship, and sharing in the fellowship meals and the prayers.
Acts 2:37–38,41–42

Children of God

Those who are led by God's Spirit are
God's sons.
The Spirit makes you God's children,
and by the Spirit's power we cry out to God,
'Father! my Father!'
From Romans 8:14–15

Written on the heart

You are the letter Christ himself wrote.
It is written, not with ink
but with the Spirit of the living God,
and not on stone tablets
but on human hearts.
From 2 Corinthians 3:2–3

Where the Spirit is

But the Spirit produces
love, joy, peace,
patience, kindness, goodness,
faithfulness, humility, and self-control.
The Spirit has given us life;
he must also control our lives.
Galatians 5:22,25

2. You belong to Christ

28 I will be with you

The eleven disciples went to the hill in Galilee
where Jesus had told them to go. When they saw
him, they worshipped him, even though some of
them doubted. Jesus drew near and said to them,

'I have been given all authority in heaven
and on earth. Go, then, to all peoples everywhere and make them my disciples: baptize
them in the name of the Father, the Son,
and the Holy Spirit, and teach them to obey
everything I have commanded you. And I
will be with you always, to the end of the
age.'
Matthew 28:16–20

29 The charge to Peter

Jesus asked his disciples, 'Who do you say I am?'
Simon Peter answered, 'You are the Messiah, the
Son of the living God.'
'Good for you, Simon son of John!' answered Jesus.
'For this truth did not come to you from any
human being, but it was given to you directly
by my Father in heaven.

And so I tell you, Peter: you are a rock, and on
this rock foundation I will build my church, and
not even death will ever be able to overcome it.
I will give you the keys of the Kingdom of heaven;
what you prohibit on earth will be prohibited in
heaven, and what you permit on earth will be
permitted in heaven.'
From Matthew 16:13–19

130 The head

I ask the God of our Lord Jesus Christ, the glorious Father, to give you the Spirit, so that your minds may be opened to see his light, and you will know what is the hope to which he has called you, how rich are the wonderful blessings he promises his people. God put all things under Christ's feet and gave him to the church as supreme Lord over all things. The church is Christ's body, the completion of him who himself completes all things everywhere.

From Ephesians 1:17–18,22–23

131 The body and its parts

We have many parts in the one body, and all these parts have different functions. In the same way, though we are many, we are one body in union with Christ, and we are all joined to each other as different parts of one body. So we are to use our different gifts in accordance with the grace that God has given us.

Romans 12:4–6

132 Becoming one

I pray that they may all be one.
Father! May they be in us,
just as you are in me and I am in you.
I gave them the same glory you gave me,
so that they may be one,
just as you and I are one.

From John 17:21–22

But you are the chosen race, the King's priests, the holy nation, God's own people, chosen to proclaim the wonderful acts of God, who called you out of darkness into his own marvellous light.

At one time you were not God's people, but now you are his people;
at one time you did not know God's mercy, but now you have received his mercy.

1 Peter 2:9–10

134 Together in joy

All the believers continued together in close fellowship and shared their belongings with one another. They would sell their property and possessions, and distribute the money among all, according to what each one needed. Day after day they met as a group in the Temple, and they had their meals together in their homes, eating with glad and humble hearts, praising God, and enjoying the good will of all the people. And every day the Lord added to their group those who were being saved.

Acts 2:44–47

Light for the whole world

You are like salt for all mankind. But if salt loses its saltiness, there is no way to make it salty again. It has become worthless, so it is thrown out and people trample on it.
You are like light for the whole world. A city built on a hill cannot be hidden. No one lights a lamp and puts it under a bowl; instead he puts it on the lampstand, where it gives light for everyone in the house. In the same way your light must shine before people, so that they will see the good things you do and praise your Father in heaven.

Matthew 5:12–16

Go!
I am sending you
like lambs among wolves.

Whoever listens to you listens to me;
whoever rejects you rejects me;
and whoever rejects me
rejects the one who sent me.

Luke 10:3,16

3. Remain in union with Christ

In him

For him

Since you have accepted
Christ Jesus as Lord,
live in union with him.
Keep your roots deep in him,
build your lives on him,
and become stronger in your faith,
as you were taught.
And be filled with thanksgiving.
Colossians 2:6–7

Anyone who is not for me is really against
me;
anyone who does not help me gather is really
scattering.
Matthew 12:30

I assure you that whoever declares publicly
that he belongs to me, the Son of Man will
do the same for him before the angels of
God.
But whoever rejects me publicly, the Son
of Man will also reject him before the angels
of God.
Luke 12:8–9

If anyone declares
that Jesus is the Son of God,
he lives in union with God
and God lives in union with him.

1 John 4:15

141

When anyone is joined to Christ,
he is a new being;
the old is gone,
the new has come.
All this is done by God,
who through Christ changed us
from enemies into his friends.

2 Corinthians 5:17–18

I am the real vine, and my Father is the gardener. Remain united to me, and I will remain united to you. A branch cannot bear fruit by itself; it can do so only if it remains in the vine. In the same way you cannot bear fruit unless you remain in me.

I am the vine, and you are the branches. Whoever remains in me, and I in him, will bear much fruit; for you can do nothing without me.

From John 15:1–5

Anyone who hears these words

So then, anyone who hears these words of mine and obeys them is like a wise man who built his house on rock.

The rain poured down, the rivers overflowed, and the wind blew hard against that house. But it did not fall, because it was built on rock.

But anyone who hears these words of mine and does not obey them is like a foolish man who built his house on sand.

The rain poured down, the rivers overflowed, the wind blew hard against that house, and it fell. And what a terrible fall that was!

Matthew 7:24–27

To have good fruit

To have good fruit you must have a healthy tree; if you have a poor tree, you will have bad fruit. A tree is known by the kind of fruit it bears. Thorn bushes do not bear grapes, and briars do not bear figs. A healthy tree bears good fruit, but a poor tree bears bad fruit.
A good person brings good things out of his treasure of good things; a bad person brings bad things out of his treasure of bad things.

From Matthew 12:33–35;16–17.

4. Because God loves us

145 The most important thing

A teacher of the Law came to Jesus with a question:
'Which commandment is the most important of all?'
Jesus replied,

'The most important one is this,
The Lord our God is the only Lord. Love the Lord your God with all your heart, with all your soul, with all your mind, and with all your strength.

The second most important commandment is this:
Love your neighbour as you love yourself.
There is no other commandment more important than these two.'

The teacher of the Law said to Jesus, 'Well done, Teacher! It is more important to obey these two commandments than to offer animals and other sacrifices to God.'
Jesus noticed how wise his answer was, and so he told him, 'You are not far from the Kingdom of God.'

From Mark 12:28–34

146 Who loves Jesus?

Whoever accepts my commandments and obeys them is the one who loves me.
My Father will love whoever loves me.
I too will love him and reveal myself to him.
My Father and I will come to him and live with him.

From John 14:21–23

Why love?

We love because God first loved us.
If someone says he loves God,
but hates his brother,
he is a liar.

For he cannot love God,
whom he has not seen,
if he does not love his brother,
whom he has seen.

The command that Christ has given us
is this: whoever loves God
must love his brother also.

1 John 4:19–21

Where love comes from

Dear friends,
let us love one another,
because love comes from God.
Whoever loves is a child of God,
for God is love.

And God showed his love for us
by sending his only Son
into the world,
so that we might have life through him.

No one has ever seen God,
but if we love one another,
God lives in union with us.

From 1 John 4:7–12

An example

It was now the day before the Passover Festival. Jesus knew that the hour had come for him to leave this world and go to the Father. He had always loved those in the world who were his own, and he loved them to the very end.

Jesus and his disciples were at supper. Jesus rose from the table, took off his outer garment, and tied a towel round his waist. Then he poured some water into a basin and began to wash the disciples' feet.

After Jesus had washed their feet, he put his outer garment back on and returned to his place at the table. 'Do you understand what I have just done to you?' he asked.

'You call me Teacher and Lord, and it is right that you do so, because that is what I am. I, your Lord and Teacher, have just washed your feet. You, then, should wash one another's feet.'

'I have set an example for you, so that you will do just what I have done for you.'

'And now I give you a new commandment: love one another. As I have loved you, so you must love one another.'

'If you have love for one another, then everyone will know that you are my disciples.'
From John 13:1–35

151 Summed up in one command

The only obligation you have
is to love one another.

All the commandments are
summed up in the one command
'Love your neighbour
as you love yourself.'

If you love someone,
you will never do him wrong;
to love is to obey the whole Law

From Romans 13:8-10

Love must be
completely sincere.

Hate what is evil,
hold on to what is good.

Be joyful,
and pray at all times.

Share your belon
with your needy
fellow-Christian

Do everything possible
on your part
to live in peace
with everybody.

Do not let evil defeat you;
instead, conquer
evil with good.

Be happy with those
that are happy,
weep with those
who weep.

Bless those who
persecute you, and
do not curse them.

How you should live 150

Do not pay back evil with evil
or cursing with cursing.

Whoever wants to enjoy life
must keep from speaking evil
and stop telling lies.

He must strive for peace
with all his heart.

From 1 Peter 3:9–11

Be kind and tender-hearted
to one another,
and forgive one another
as God has forgiven you
through Christ.

Ephesians 4:32

5. Asking and praying

152 On his own

But he would go away to lonely places, where he prayed.
Luke 5:16

At that time Jesus went up a hill to pray and spent the whole night there praying to God.
Luke 6:12

How you should pray

Our Father in heaven:

May your holy name be honoured;
may your Kingdom come;
may your will be done
on earth as it is in heaven.

Give us today the food we need.
Forgive us the wrongs we have done,
as we forgive the wrongs
that others have done to us.
Do not bring us to hard testing,
but keep us safe from the Evil One.

Matthew 6:9–13

54 Do not use meaningless words

When you pray, do not use a lot of meaningless words, as the pagans do, who think that God will hear them because their prayers are long. Do not be like them. Your Father already knows what you need before you ask him.
Matthew 6:7–8

55 Not like the hypocrites

When you pray, do not be like the hypocrites! They love to stand up and pray in the houses of worship and on the street corners, so that everyone will see them. I assure you, they have already been paid in full. But when you pray, go to your room, close the door, and pray to your Father, who is unseen. And your Father, who sees what you do in private, will reward you.
Matthew 6:5–6

56 Keep on asking

And Jesus said to his disciples, 'Suppose one of you should go to a friend's house at midnight and say to him, "Friend, let me borrow three loaves of bread. A friend of mine who is on a journey has just come to my house, and I haven't got any food for him!" And suppose your friend should answer from inside, "Don't bother me! The door is already locked, and my children and I are in bed. I can't get up and give you anything." Well, what then? I tell you that even if he will not get up and give you the bread because you are his friend, yet he will get up and give you everything you need because you are not ashamed to keep on asking.'
Luke 11:5–8

Pray together 157

And I tell you more:
whenever two of you on earth
agree about anything you pray for,
it will be done for you
by my Father in heaven.
For where two or three come together
in my name,
I am there with them.
Matthew 18:19–20

Ask 158

Ask, and you will receive; seek, and you will find; knock, and the door will be opened to you.

Would any of you who are fathers give your son a stone when he asks for bread? Or would you give him a snake when he asks for a fish?

Bad as you are, you know how to give good things to your children. How much more, then, will your Father in heaven give good things to those who ask him!
From Matthew 7:7–11

6. When alone and afraid

Alone

1

My Lord, our King, the only one,
come to my help,
for I am alone
and have no helper but you

O God,
whose strength prevails over all
free me from my fear.
From Esther 4:17,19

How much longer?

1

How much longer
will you forget me, LORD?
For ever?
How much longer
will you hide yourself from me?

Look at me, O LORD my God,
and answer me.
Restore my strength;
don't let me die.

I rely on your constant love;
I will be glad,
because you will rescue me,
I will sing to you, O LORD,
because you have been good to me.
From Psalm 13

I look to the mountains;
where will my help come from?

My help will come from the LORD,
who made heaven and earth.

He will not let you fall;
your protector is always awake.

The LORD will guard you;
he is by your side to protect you.

The LORD will protect you from all danger;
he will keep you safe.

He will protect you as you come and go
now and for ever.
From Psalm 121

161   Why are you frightened?

Jesus said to his disciples, 'Let us go across to
the other side of the lake.' So they left the crowd.
Suddenly a strong wind blew up, and the waves
began to spill over into the boat, so that it was
about to fill with water.
Jesus was in the back of the boat, sleeping with
his head on a pillow. The disciples woke him up
and said, 'Teacher, don't you care that we are
about to die?'
Jesus stood up and commanded the wind, 'Be
quiet!' and he said to the waves, 'Be still!' The
wind died down, and there was a great calm. Then
Jesus said to his disciples, 'Why are you frightened?
Have you still no faith?'
But they were terribly afraid and said to one
another, 'Who is this man? Even the wind and
the waves obey him!'
Mark 4:35–41

7. When you are worried

163 Look at the crows

And so I tell you not to worry about the food you need to stay alive or about the clothes you need for your body. Life is much more important than food, and the body much more important than clothes. Look at the crows: they don't sow seeds or gather a harvest; they don't have store-rooms or barns; God feeds them! You are worth so much more than birds!

Luke 12:22–24

Why worry?

Can any of you live a bit longer by worrying about it? If you can't manage even such a small thing, why worry about the other things?

Luke 12:25–26

Look at the flowers

Look how the wild flowers grow: they don't work or make clothes for themselves. But I tell you that not even King Solomon with all his wealth had clothes as beautiful as one of these flowers. It is God who clothes the wild grass – grass that is here today and gone tomorrow, burnt up in the oven. Won't he be all the more sure to clothe you? How little faith you have!

Luke 12:27–28

Don't be upset

So don't be all upset, always concerned about what you will eat and drink.
Your Father knows that you need these things. Instead, be concerned with his Kingdom, and he will provide you with these things.

From Luke 12:29–31

No one can be a slave of two masters;
he will hate one and love the other;
he will be loyal to one and despise the
other.
You cannot serve both God and money.
Matthew 6:24

Where your heart will be

Do not store up riches for yourselves here on earth,
where moths and rust destroy, and robbers break
in and steal.

Instead, store up riches for yourselves in heaven,
where moths and rust cannot destroy, and robbers
cannot break in and steal. For your heart will
always be where your riches are.
Matthew 6:19–21

What's the use?

16

Then Jesus told them this parable: 'There was
once a rich man who had land which bore good
crops. He began to think to himself, "I haven't
anywhere to keep all my crops. What can I do?
This is what I will do," he told himself; "I will
tear down my barns and build bigger ones, where
I will store my corn and all my other goods. Then
I will say to myself, Lucky man! You have all
the good things you need for many years. Take
life easy, eat, drink, and enjoy yourself!"
But God said to him, "You fool! This very night
you will have to give up your life; then who will
get all these things you have kept for yourself?"'
And Jesus concluded, 'This is how it is with those
who pile up riches for themselves but are not rich
in God's sight.'
Luke 12:16–21

8. Friends and enemies

70 Friends

Two are better off than one, because together they can work more effectively. If one of them falls down, the other can help him up.

But if someone is alone and falls, it's just too bad, because there is no one to help him.

Ecclesiastes 4:9–10

171

If you want to make a friend,
take him on trial.

A faithful friend is a sure shelter,
whoever finds one has found a rare treasure.

A faithful friend is something beyond price,
there is no measuring his worth.

Ecclesiasticus 6:7,14–15

The start of an argument

172

The start of an argument is like the first break in a dam; stop it before it goes any further.

Proverbs 17:14

Don't make friends with people who have hot, violent tempers. You might learn their habits and not be able to change.

Proverbs 22:24–25

Don't take it on yourself to repay a wrong. Trust the LORD and he will make it right.

Proverbs 20:22

Be merciful to me, O God,
because I am under attack.
My enemies persecute me all the time.

All day long my opponents attack me.
There are so many who fight against me.

When I am afraid, O LORD Almighty,
I put my trust in you.
I trust in God and am not afraid;
I praise him for what he has promised.
What can a mere human being do to me?

You know how troubled I am;
you have kept a record of my tears.
Aren't they listed in your book?

The day I call to you,
My enemies will be turned back.

I know this: God is on my side –
the LORD, whose promises I praise.
In him I trust, and I will not be afraid.
What can a mere human being do to me?
Psalm 56:1–4,8–11.

173 They are for war

When I was in trouble,
I called to the LORD.
Save me, LORD,
from liars and deceivers.
I have lived too long
with people who hate peace!
When I speak of peace,
they are for war.
From Psalm 120

You have heard that it was said,
'Love your friends,
hate your enemies.'
But now I tell you:
love your enemies
and pray for those who persecute you,
so that you may become the sons
of your Father in heaven.
For he makes his sun to shine
on bad and good people alike,
and gives rain to those who do good
and to those who do evil.

Matthew 5:43–45

Jesus set out on his way to Jerusalem, and went into a village in Samaria. But the people there would not receive him. When the disciples James and John saw this, they said, 'Lord, do you want us to call fire down from heaven to destroy them?' Jesus turned and rebuked them, and said, 'You don't know what kind of a Spirit you belong to; for the Son of Man did not come to destroy men's lives, but to save them.' Then Jesus and his disciples went on to another village.

From Luke 9:51–56

177 You should have had mercy

'The Kingdom of heaven is like this. Once there was a king who decided to check on his servants' accounts. He had just begun to do so when one of them was brought in who owed him millions of pounds. The servant did not have enough to pay his debt, so the king ordered him to be sold as a slave, with his wife and his children and all that he had, in order to pay the debt. The servant fell on his knees before the king. "Be patient with me," he begged, "and I will pay you everything!" The king felt sorry for him, so he forgave him the debt and let him go.'

'Then the man went out and met one of his fellow-servants who owed him a few pounds. He grabbed him and started choking him. "Pay back what you owe me!" he said. His fellow-servant fell down and begged him, "Be patient with me, and I will pay you back!" But he refused; instead, he had him thrown into jail until he should pay the debt.

When the other servants saw what had happened, they were very upset and went to the king and told him everything. So he called the servant in. "You worthless slave!" he said. "I forgave you the whole amount you owed me, just because you asked me to. You should have had mercy on your fellow-servant, just as I had mercy on you." The king was very angry, and he sent the servant to jail to be punished until he should pay back the whole amount.'

And Jesus concluded, 'That is how my father in heaven will treat every one of you unless you forgive your brother from your heart.'

Matthew 18:23-35

How often?

17

If your brother sins, rebuke him, and if he repents, forgive him. If he sins against you seven times in one day, and each time he comes to you saying, 'I repent,' you must forgive him.　　　Luke 17:3-4

179 So there can be peace

Be always humble, gentle, and patient. Show your love by being tolerant with one another. Do your best to preserve the unity which the Spirit gives by means of the peace that binds you together.

Ephesians 4:2-3

Be tolerant with one another and forgive one another. You must forgive one another just as the Lord has forgiven you. And to these qualities add love, which binds all things together in perfect unity. The peace that Christ gives is to guide you in the decisions you make.

From Colossians 3:13-15

80 He endured suffering

We despised him and rejected him;
he endured suffering and pain.
No one would even look at him—
we ignored him as if he was nothing.

He was treated harshly, but endured it humbly;
he never said a word.
Like a lamb about to be slaughtered,
like a sheep about to be sheared,
he never said a word.

Isaiah 53:3,7

Then he breathed on them and said, 'Receive the Holy Spirit. If you forgive people's sins, they are forgiven; if you do not forgive them, they are not forgiven.'

John 20:19–23

With his own body 18

For Christ himself has brought us peace by making us one people. With his own body he broke down the wall that separated us and kept us enemies. By his death on the cross Christ destroyed our enmity. He came and preached the Good News of peace to all.

From Ephesians 2:14,16–17

May God our Father and the Lord Jesus Christ give you grace and peace.

1 Corinthians 1:3

May God, our source of peace, be with all of you. Amen.

Romans 15:33

181 If you forgive people's sins

It was late Sunday evening, and the disciples were gathered together behind locked doors, because they were afraid of the Jewish authorities.

Then Jesus came and stood among them. 'Peace be with you,' he said. After saying this, he showed them his hands and his side. The disciples were filled with joy at seeing the Lord.

Jesus said to them again, 'Peace be with you. As the Father sent me, so I send you.'

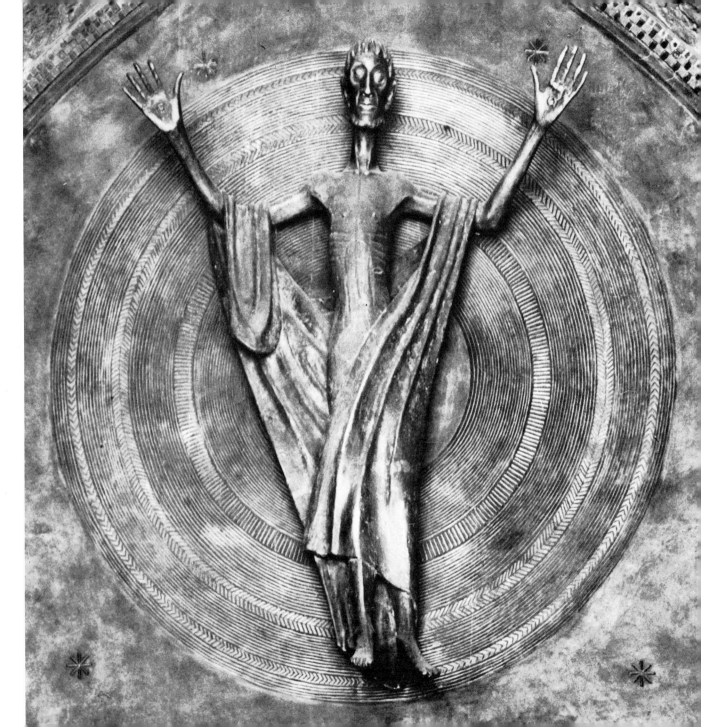

9. Sin, repentance and forgiveness

183 Forsaking the spring of fresh water

My people have committed two sins:
they have turned away from me,
the spring of fresh water,
and they have dug cisterns,
cracked cisterns
that can hold no water at all.
Jeremiah 2:13

They will not give up their sinning 18

The LORD says, 'My people do one evil thing
after another, and do not acknowledge me
as their God.'
Everyone must be on guard against his
friend, and no one can trust his brother;
for everyone slanders his friends. They all
mislead their friends, and no one tells the
truth; they have taught their tongues to lie
and will not give up their sinning. They
do one violent thing after another, and one
deceitful act follows another.
From Jeremiah 9:3–5

185 Filled with wickedness

Because people refuse to keep in mind the true knowledge about God, he has given them over to currupted minds, so that they do the things that they should not do.

They are filled with all kinds of wickedness, evil, greed, and vice; they are full of jealousy, murder, fighting, deceit, and malice. They gossip and speak evil of one another; they are hateful to God, insolent, proud, and boastful; they think of more ways to do evil; they disobey their parents; they have no conscience; they do not keep their promises, and they show no kindness or pity for others.

Romans 1:28–31

186 Their minds are dull

This people will listen and listen,
but not understand;
they will look and look,
but not see,
because their minds are dull,
and they have stopped up their ears
and have closed their eyes.

Matthew 13:14–15

They did not receive Christ

187

The Word was in the world, and though God made the world through him, yet the world did not recognize him. He came to his own country, but his own people did not receive him.

John 1:10–11

188

The light has come into the world, but people love the darkness rather than the light, because their deeds are evil.

Anyone who does evil things hates the light and will not come to the light, because he does not want his evil deeds to be shown up.

John 3:19–20

189

They are wrong about sin and about what is right, because they do not believe in me.

From John 16:8–9

Joy in heaven

One day when many tax collectors and other outcasts came to listen to Jesus, the Pharisees and the teachers of the Law started grumbling, 'This man welcomes outcasts and even eats with them!' So Jesus told them this parable:

'Suppose one of you has a hundred sheep and loses one of them – what does he do? He leaves the other ninety-nine sheep in the pasture and goes looking for the one that got lost until he finds it. When he finds it, he is so happy that he puts it on his shoulders and carries it back home. Then he calls his friends and neighbours together and says to them, "I am so happy I found my lost sheep. Let us celebrate!" In the same way, I tell you, there will be more joy in heaven over one sinner who repents than over ninety-nine respectable people who do not need to repent.'   Luke 15:1–7

Greater than sin

I am the high and holy God, who lives for ever. I gave my people life. I was angry with them because of their sin and greed, and so I punished them and abandoned them. But they were stubborn and kept on going their own way.

I have seen how they acted, but I will heal them. I will lead them and help them, and I will comfort those who mourn. I offer peace to all, both near and far! I will heal my people.

From Isaiah 57:15–19

Suppose a woman who has ten silver coins loses one of them – what does she do? She lights a lamp, sweeps her house, and looks carefully everywhere until she finds it. When she finds it, she calls her friends and neighbours together, and says to them,

'I am so happy I found the coin I lost. Let us celebrate!'

In the same way, I tell you, the angels of God rejoice over one sinner who repents.

Luke 15:8–10

Praise the LORD, my soul,
and do not forget how kind he is.

He forgives all my sins
and heals all my diseases.

The LORD is merciful and loving,
slow to become angry and full of constant love.

He does not punish us as we deserve
or repay us for our sins and wrongs.

As high as the sky is above the earth,
so great is his love for those who honour him.

From Psalm 103:2–11

get up and go to my father and say, Father, I have sinned against God and against you. I am no longer fit to be called your son." So he got up and started back to his father.

'He was still a long way from home when his father saw him; his heart was filled with pity, and he ran, threw his arms round his son, and kissed him. "Father," the son said, "I have sinned against God and against you. I am no longer fit to be called your·son." But the father called his servants. "Hurry!" he said. "Bring the best robe and put it on him. Then go and get the prize calf and kill it, and let us celebrate with a feast! For this son of mine was dead, but now he is alive; he was lost, but now he has been found."'

From Luke 15:11–24

You are merciful to all

Or perhaps you despise his great kindness, tolerance, and patience. Surely you know that God is kind, because he is trying to lead you to repent.

Romans 2:4

Your great strength is always at your call; who can withstand the might of your arm? Yet you are merciful to all, because you can do all things and overlook men's sins so that they can repent.

From Wisdom 11:21–24

194 He ran towards him

Jesus said, 'There was once a man who had two sons. The younger one said to him, "Father, give me my share of the property now." So the man divided his property between his two sons. After a few days the younger son sold his part of the property and left home with the money. He went to a country far away, where he wasted his money in reckless living. He spent everything he had. Then a severe famine spread over that country, and he was left without a thing. So he went to work for one of the citizens of that country, who sent him out to his farm to take care of the pigs. He wished he could fill himself with the bean pods the pigs ate, but no one gave him anything to eat. At last he came to his senses and said, "All my father's hired workers have more than they can eat, and here I am about to starve! I will

97 God, have pity on me, a sinner!

Jesus also told this parable to people who were sure of their own goodness and despised everybody else. 'Once there were two men who went up to the Temple to pray: one was a Pharisee, the other a tax collector.
The Pharisee prayed, "I thank you, God, that I am not greedy, dishonest, or an adulterer, like everybody else. I thank you that I am not like that tax collector over there." But the tax collector stood at a distance and would not even raise his face to heaven, but beat on his breast and said, "God, have pity on me, a sinner!"
'I tell you,' said Jesus, 'the tax collector, and not the Pharisee, was in the right with God when he went home.'

Luke 18:9–14

If we confess our sins 198

If we say that we have no sin, we deceive ourselves, and there is no truth in us.

But if we confess our sins to God, he will keep his promise and do what is right: he will forgive us our sins and purify us from all our wrongdoing.

1 John 1:8–9

199

Happy are those whose sins are forgiven, whose wrongs are pardoned.
Happy is the man whom the LORD does not accuse of doing wrong
and who is free from all deceit.
When I did not confess my sins,
I was worn out from crying all day long.
Then I confessed my sins to you;
I did not conceal my wrongdoings.
I decided to confess them to you,
and you forgave all my sins.

From Psalm 32:1–5

200 Whoever has committed no sin

The teachers of the Law and the Pharisees brought in a woman who had been caught committing adultery. 'Teacher,' they said to Jesus, 'Moses commanded that such a woman must be stoned to death. Now, what do you say?' He said to them, 'Whichever one of you has commited no sin may throw the first stone at her.' When they heard this, they all left, one by one, the older ones first. Jesus was left alone, with the woman still standing there. 'I do not condemn you,' Jesus said. 'Go, but do not sin again.'   From John 8:3-11

201 Seeking the lost

There was a chief tax collector named Zacchaeus, who was rich. He was a little man and could not see Jesus because of the crowd. So he ran ahead and climbed a sycamore tree to see Jesus, who was going to pass that way. When Jesus came to that place, he looked up and said to Zacchaeus, 'Hurry down, Zacchaeus, because I must stay in your house today.'
Zacchaeus hurried down and welcomed him with great joy. All the people who saw it started grumbling, 'This man has gone as a guest to the home of a sinner!'
Zacchaeus stood up and said to the Lord, 'Listen, sir! I will give half my belongings to the poor, and if I have cheated anyone, I will pay him back four times as much.'
Jesus said to him, 'Salvation has come to this house today, for this man, also, is a descendant of Abraham. The Son of Man came to seek and to save the lost.'   Luke 19:1-10

202 See yourself for what you are

God will judge you in the same way as you judge others, and he will apply to you the same rules you apply to others. Why, then, do you look at the speck in your brother's eye, and pay no attention to the log in your own eye? How dare you say to your brother, 'Please, let me take that speck out of your eye,' when you have a log in your own eye? You hypocrite! First take the log out of your own eye, and then you will be able to see clearly to take the speck out of your brother's eye.
Matthew 7:2-5

Put on the new self

203

Get rid of your old self, which made you live as you used to. Your hearts and minds must be made completely new, and you must put on the new self, which is created in God's likeness.

No more lying, then! Everyone must tell the truth. The man who used to rob must stop robbing and start working, in order to earn an honest living for himself and to be able to help the poor.
From Ephesians 4:22-25,28

204

If you will turn back to the LORD and with all your heart obey his commands, then the LORD your God will have mercy on you.
From Deuteronomy 30:2-3

10. God is ahead of us

No more than a shadow

Dying

How short you have made my life!
In your sight my lifetime seems nothing.
Indeed every living man is no more than
a puff of wind,
no more than a shadow.
All he does is for nothing;
he gathers wealth,
but doesn't know who will get it.
What, then, can I hope for, Lord?
I put my hope in you.
Save me from all my sins.
Psalm 39:5–8

You tell man to return to what he was;
you change him back to dust.
A thousand years to you are like one day.
We are like weeds that sprout in the morning,
that grow and burst into bloom,
then dry up and die in the evening.
Seventy years is all we have – eighty years,
if we are strong;

Lord our God, may your blessings be with
us.
Give us success in all we do!
From Psalm 90:3–17

207 Is everything useless?

Life is useless, all useless.
You spend your life working, labouring,
and what do you have to show for it?

Generations come and generations go,
but the world stays just the same.

The sun still rises,
and it still goes down.
There is nothing new in the whole world.

I determined that I would study
all the things that are done in this world,
and I tell you,
it is all useless.
It is like chasing the wind.

I decided to enjoy myself
and find out what happiness is.
Driven on by my desire for wisdom,
I decided to cheer myself up with wine
and have a good time.
But I found that this is useless, too.

I accomplished great things.
I built myself houses and planted vineyards.
I bought many slaves,
and I also piled up silver and gold.
Then I thought about all that I had done
and how hard I had worked doing it,
and I realized that it didn't mean a thing.
It was like chasing the wind.

I looked at all the injustice
that goes on in this world.
The oppressed were weeping,
and no one would help them.
But it is useless.

After all this,
there is only one thing to say:
Fear God,
and obey his commands.
God is going to judge everything we do,
whether good or bad.
From Ecclesiastes 1,2,4,12

115

You will cry and weep, but the world will be glad; you will be sad, but your sadness will turn into gladness.

When a woman is about to give birth, she is sad because her hour of suffering has come; but when the baby is born, she forgets her suffering, because she is happy that a baby has been born into the world.

That is how it is with you: now you are sad, but I will see you again, and your hearts will be filled with gladness, the kind of gladness that no one can take away from you.
John 16:20–22

208 We wait to be set free

I consider that what we suffer at this present time cannot be compared at all with the glory that is going to be revealed to us. All of creation waits with eager longing for God to reveal his sons. For creation was condemned to lose its purpose, not of its own will, but because God willed it to be so. Yet there was the hope that creation itself would one day be set free from its slavery to decay and would share the glorious freedom of the children of God. For we know that up to the present time all of creation groans with pain, like the pain of childbirth. But it is not just creation alone which groans; we who have the Spirit as the first of God's gifts also groan within ourselves, as we wait for God to make us his sons and set our whole being free.
Romans 8:18–23

Because of his love God had already decided that through Jesus Christ he would make us his sons – this was his pleasure and purpose. Let us praise God for his glorious grace, for the free gift he gave us in his dear Son! For by the death of Christ we are set free, that is, our sins are forgiven. How great is the grace of God, which he gave to us in such large measure!
Ephesians 1:4–8

The guarantee

210

Now, since our message is that Christ has been raised from death, how can some of you say that the dead will not be raised to life?

And if Christ has not been raised, then your faith is a delusion and you are still lost in your sins.

But the truth is that Christ has been raised from death, as the guarantee that those who sleep in death will also be raised.

1 Corinthians 15:12,17,20

I am filled with gladness

211

I saw the Lord before me at all times;
he is near me,
and I will not be troubled.
And so I am filled with gladness,
and my words are full of joy.

And I, mortal though I am,
will rest assured in hope,
because you will not abandon me
in the world of the dead.

You have shown me the paths
that lead to life,
and your presence will fill me with joy.

From Acts 2:25–28

When the Son of Man comes as King and all the angels with him, he will sit on his royal throne, and the people of all the nations will be gathered before him. Then he will divide them into two groups, just as a shepherd separates the sheep from the goats. He will put the righteous people on his right and the others on his left. Then the King will say to the people on his right,

'Come, you that are blessed by my Father!
Come and possess the kingdom
which has been prepared for you
ever since the creation of the world.
I was hungry and you fed me,
thirsty and you gave me a drink;
I was a stranger
and you received me in your homes,
naked and you clothed me;
I was sick and you took care of me,
in prison and you visited me.'

The righteous will then answer him,
'When, Lord, did we ever see you
hungry and feed you,
or thirsty and give you a drink?
When did we ever see you a stranger
and welcome you in our homes,
or naked and clothe you?
When did we ever see you sick
or in prison, and visit you?'

The King will reply,
'I tell you, whenever you did this for one of the least important of these brothers of mine, you did it for me!'   Matthew 25:31–40

Jesus told them another parable: 'The Kingdom of heaven is like this. A man sowed good seed in his field. One night, when everyone was asleep, an enemy came and sowed weeds among the wheat and went away. When the plants grew and the ears of corn began to form, then the weeds showed up. The man's servants came to him and said, "Sir, it was good seed you sowed in your field; where did the weeds come from?" "It was some enemy who did this," he answered. "Do you want us to go and pull up the weeds?" they asked him. "No," he answered, "because as you gather the weeds you might pull up some of the wheat along with them. Let the wheat and the weeds both grow together until harvest. Then I will tell the harvest workers to pull up the weeds first, tie them in bundles and burn them, and then to gather in the wheat and put it in my barn."

'The man who sowed the good seed is the Son of Man; the field is the world; the good seed is the people who belong to the Kingdom; the weeds are the people who belong to the Evil One; and the enemy who sowed the weeds is the Devil. The harvest is the end of the age, and the harvest workers are angels. Just as the weeds are gathered up and burnt in the fire, so the same thing will happen at the end of the age.'
Matthew 13:24–30,37–40

214 We shall see him

For our gifts of knowledge and of inspired messages
are only partial;
but when what is perfect comes,
then what is partial will disappear.

What we see now is like a dim image in a mirror;
then we shall see face to face.

What I know now is only partial;
then it will be complete –
as complete as God's knowledge of me.

1 Corinthians 13:9–10,12

215

And eternal life
means knowing you,
the only true God,
and knowing Jesus Christ,
whom you sent.

John 17:3

What awaits us 21

What no one ever saw or heard,
what no one ever thought could happen,
is the very thing God prepared
for those who love him.

1 Corinthians 2:9

I make all things new 21

Then I saw a new heaven and a new earth. The
first heaven and the first earth disappeared, and
the sea vanished. And I saw the Holy City, the
new Jerusalem, coming down out of heaven from
God, prepared and ready, like a bride dressed to
meet her husband. I heard a loud voice speaking
from the throne: 'Now God's home is with mankind! He will live with them, and they shall be
his people. God himself will be with them, and
he will be their God. He will wipe away all tears
from their eyes. There will be no more death,
no more grief or crying or pain. The old things
have disappeared.' Then the one who sits on the
throne said, 'And now I make all things new!'

Revelation 21:1–5

218

The full nature of God

Christ is the visible likeness
of the invisible God.
He is the first-born Son,
superior to all created things.

For through him God created
everything in heaven and on earth,
the seen and the unseen things.
God created the whole universe
through him and for him.
Christ existed before all things.

He is the head of his body, the church;
he is the source of the body's life.

He is the first-born Son,
who was raised from death,
in order that he alone
might have the first place in all things.

For it was by God's own decision
that the Son has in himself
the full nature of God.

God made peace
through his Son's death on the cross
and so brought back to himself all things,
both on earth and in heaven.

From Colossians 1:15—20

An Appreciation
by F. F. Bruce

BIBLE FOR TODAY is based on a twofold conviction about religious education. First, in our culture where religious education is essentially Christian, it must be founded on an intelligent grasp of the Bible. Secondly, it must be related to the experience of children and youth.

This means that the task of religious education is to illuminate and interpret the meaning of life in the light of the Christian faith. It is to present that faith in the context of today's world, and an indispensable part of the learning process is the study of those experiences of God, of human beings and of the world in general which are found in the Bible. This selection of texts has been made in order to bring out these experiences and show their relevance to the experiences of life today.

Most Bibles aimed at young people present their choice of passages historically. In large measure *Bible for Today* has followed this precedent. Man's understanding of God has come in the course of history; the biblical revelation was not only given in the context of history but was closely bound up with that historical context. The events which the Bible records are historical events. Therefore in Parts I and II we have followed the traditional division of the Bible into the Old and New Testaments, corresponding to the two main phases in the history of salvation. By this means the ways of God with men and women can be made clear.

But something is necessary over and above the historical arrangement. Some young people very often lack historical perspective; any gripping story from the past is visualized by them as belonging to the present. Therefore Part III has been included: here the historical arrangement is supplemented by an arrangement of texts from both

Testaments based on themes and experiences. It has been proved that such an arrangement can make the message of the Bible alive and relevant in a surprisingly new way.

From this selection many readers will want to make a selection of their own; some may be encouraged to make an alternative or additional selection to cover questions which arise from time to time and which appear to be given no adequate answer in this selection.

To ensure the utmost flexibility, we have refrained almost entirely from adding explanatory notes. We have not even drawn up sets of questions for further study, preferring that readers and study groups should consider those questions which are of greatest actual urgency to themselves.

The use of the selections will be helped by the two indices – an index of Bible references and an alphabetical index of subjects. But these indices are intended only as a guide. Many texts are listed several times because they can be used in a variety of ways, and readers of *Bible for Today* may think of further ways in which they can be used.

The text is chiefly that of the Good News Bible – a modern English version admirably suited to the needs and interests of young people.

I can assure parents and teachers who wish to create an interest in the teachings of the Bible that what they have here is a most useful tool, though many who are not so young will also find the selection of passages and the illustrative artwork stimulating.

Contents

I.   A NATION ENCOUNTERS GOD

1 God was not invented by men   5
Psa. 90:2

1. The God who cannot be comprehended

2 God cannot be compared with anything   6
Psa. 89:8–9

3 God's thoughts are not ours   6
Isa. 55:8–9

4 God is like a riddle   6
Psa. 139:17–18

5 God may not be seen   7
Ex. 33:18–23

6 No one is like God   8
Isa. 40:12,15,17,18

7 How great is your strength!   9
From Psa. 89:9–17

2. God has set us free

8 This our God has done   10
Deut. 26:5–9

9 I am who I am   11
From Ex. 2:23–24; 3:1–17

10 God has saved us   12
From Ex. 14

11 The song of victory at the Red Sea   13
From Ex. 15:1–13

3. He is with us

12 He cares about us   14
From Ex. 16:1–15

13 God is like a father   15
Psa. 103:13,17–18

14 God is like a mother   15
Isa. 49:15

15 God is like a shepherd   16
Isa. 40:10–11

16 Psa. 23:1–2,4   16

4. A covenant with God

17 I will be your God   17
Lev. 26:9, 11–12

18 You will be my people   17
From Ex. 19: 1–8

19 You will have all you want   19
Deut. 8:7–10

20 You have given us everything   19
From Psa. 104

21 Chosen because he loves us   19
Deut. 7:6–9

5. From the beginning

22 From Gen. 12:1–4   20

23 Gen. 13:14–18   20

24 Gen. 15:1–6   21

25 Gen. 17:1–8   21

26 From Gen. 18:1–16   21

27 From Gen. 21:1–7   21

28 I will not leave you   22
Gen. 28:10–19

29 From Gen. 32:22–30   22

6. It is what God wants

30 What God demands   23
Deut. 10:12–13

31 The LORD alone   23
Deut. 6:4–5

32 Ten signposts point the way   24
From Deut. 5:6–21

33 I am the LORD your God   24
From Lev. 19:9–18

34 Like a son to the Most High   25
From Ecclus. 4:1–11

35 From Ecclus. 3:6–8   25

7. God's world is for you

36 Praise the Lord!   27
From Psa. 148

37 To govern the world   27
From Wis. 9:1–4

38 How great you are   28
From Psa. 8

8. God is our king

39 The king: the anointed one   29
From 1 Sam. 16:6–13

40 The king: 'a son of God'   30
Psa. 2:7,10–12

41 In the name of the God of Israel . . .   30
From 1 Sam. 17

42 You have disobeyed my commands   31
From 2 Sam. 11 and 12

9. Return to God

43 You have turned your backs   32
From Isa. 1:2–4

44 They refuse to return   33
From Hosea 11:1–5

45 Return to the LORD   33
From Hosea 14:2–5

46 Proclaim what I command you   34
From Jer. 1:4–9,16–19

47 Come back to me!   34
From Jer. 3:12–13

48 You are this vineyard   35
From Isa. 5:1–7

10. God will come

49 A new way   36
From Isa. 40:1–5

50 A new covenant   36
From Jer. 31:31–34

51 A new heart   37
From Ezek. 36:26–28

52 A new shepherd   37
From Ezek. 34:1–6,11,16,23

53 The Messiah   38
From Isa. 11:2–4

54 From Isa. 9:2–7   38

55 How it will be in God's Kingdom   38
Micah 4:3–4

56 Isa. 11:6–9   38

57 From Isa. 25:6–8   38

58 Encounters with God   40
From the prayers of Israel

II. GOD: IN JESUS

59 So that our joy may be complete ... 41
From 1 John 1:1–4

1. He is the Christ

60 You will give birth to a son 42
From Luke 1:26–38

61 Christ the Lord 42
From Luke 2:1–18

62 They fell down before him 44
From Matt. 2:1–12

2. We have found him

63 Get the road ready for the Lord 45
From Luke 3:1–9

64 He comes after me 45
From John 1:19–27

65 We have found the Messiah 46
From John 1:35–39

66 John 1:40–41 46

67 Out of Nazareth 46
John 1:43–50

68 From now on you will be catching men 47
From Luke 5:1–11

69 Follow me 47
Luke 5:27–32

3. They were astonished at his teaching

70 The Kingdom of God 48
Mark 1:14–15

71 They were amazed 48
Mark 1:21–22

72 They took offence at him 48
From Mark 6:1–6

73 From Luke 4:16–24,28–30 48

74 Good News 49
From Matt. 4:23–5:10

75 Who belongs to Jesus? 50
From Mark 3:31–35

76 Who is the greatest? 50
Mark 9:33–37

77 Who gave more? 50
Mark 12:41–44

78 Who is the greatest? 50
Luke 22:24–27

79 To whom does the Kingdom of God belong? 51
Mark 10:13–16

80 When will the Kingdom of God come? 51
Luke 17:20–21

81 What must I do? 52
Luke 10:25–28

82 Who is my neighbour? 52
Luke 10:29–37

83 Who bears good fruit? 53
From Matt. 13:1–9,18–23

84 What is the Kingdom of heaven like? 54
Matt. 13:44

85 Matt. 13:45 54

86 Matt. 13:33 54

87 What is the Kingdom of heaven like? 55
Matt. 13:31–32

4. He can heal anyone

88 Be opened 56
From Mark 7:32–37

89 Sir, if you want to 56
Matt. 8:2–3

90 Take pity on me 56
Mark 10:46–52

91 Just give the order 57
From Luke 7:1–10

92 His heart was filled with pity 57
Luke 7:11–16

93 Who can forgive sins? 57
Mark 2:1–12

94 Are you the one who is to come? 59
Luke 7:18–22

5. Who is this man?

95 Because he called God his father . . . 60
From John 5:1–18

96 The Prophet? 60
From John 6:1–15

97 Whoever eats me 60
From John 6:22–69

98 They quarrelled about him 62
From John 7:10–12

99 How does this man know so much? 62
John 7:14–16

100 Is he the Messiah? 62
John 7:40–47

101 Who are you? 62
From John 10:22–39

6. My life – for you

102 God bless the king! 64
From Luke 19:28–38

103 They tried to find a way 64
From Luke 22:1–6

104 My body – for you 65
From Luke 22:7–20

105 In great anguish 66
From Luke 22:39–46

106 Betrayed! 66
From Luke 22:47–53

107 Beaten 67
From Luke 22:54,63–71

108 Accused 67
From Luke 23:1–11

109 Condemned 67
From Luke 23:13–16,21–24

110 Dead 69
From Luke 23:26,32–38,44–46

111 Buried 69
Luke 23:50–54

7. He lives

112 The guarantee 70
From 1 Cor. 15:1–8,20

113 He has been raised! 70
Mark 16:1–8

114 Then their eyes were opened 71
From Luke 24:13–31

115 Feel me! 71
From Luke 24:36–43

116 My Lord and my God! 73
John 20:24–29

117 Be glad 73
From John 14:27–28

118 Taken up to heaven 74
From Acts 1:8–11

119 God has made him Lord 74
From Eph. 1:3,20–22

120 John 21:25 74

121 Jesus Christ is Lord 74
From Phil. 2:6–11

III.   GOD: IN THE MIDST OF US

1. The Spirit of Jesus

122 They were filled with the Holy Spirit 77
Acts 2:1–4

123 What does this mean? 78
From Acts 2:6–33

124 What shall we do? 78
Acts 2:37–38,41–42

125 Children of God 79
From Rom. 8:14–15

126 Written on the heart 79
From 2 Cor. 3:2–3

127 Where the Spirit is 79
Gal. 5:22,25

2. You belong to Christ

128 I will be with you 81
Matt. 28:16–20

129 The charge to Peter 81
From Matt. 16:13–19

130 The head 82
From Eph. 1:17:18,22–23

131 The body and its parts 82
Rom. 12:4–6

132 Becoming one 82
From John 17:21–22

133 God's own people 83
1 Peter 2:9–10

134 Together in joy 83
Acts 2:44–47

135 Light for the whole world 83
Matt. 5:12–16

136 Luke 10:3,16 83

3. Remain in union with Christ

137 In him 84
Col. 2:6–7

138 For him 84
Matt. 12:30

139 Luke 12:8–9 84

140 With him 85
1 John 4:15

141 2 Cor. 5:17–18 85

142 Remain united to me 85
From John 15:1–5

143 Anyone who hears these words 87
Matt. 7:24–27

144 To have good fruit 87
From Matt. 12:33–35; 7:16–17

4. Because God loves us

145 The most important thing 88
From Mark 12:28–34

146 Who loves Jesus? 88
From John 14:21–23

147 Why love? 88
1 John 4:19–21

148 Where love comes from 88
From 1 John 4:7–12

149 An example 89
From John 13:1–35

150 How you should live 90
From 1 Peter 3:9–11 and Eph. 4:32

151 Summed up in the one command 90
Rom. 13:8–10

5. Asking and praying

152 On his own 92
Luke 5:16 and Luke 6:12

153 How you should pray 92
Matt. 6:9–13

154 Do not use meaningless words 93
Matt. 6:7–8

155 Not like the hypocrites 93
Matt. 6:5–6

156 Keep on asking 93
Luke 11:5–8

157 Pray together 93
Matt. 18:19–20

158 Ask 93
From Matt. 7:7–11

6. When alone and afraid

159 Alone 94
From Esther 4:17,19

160 How much longer? 94
From Psa. 13

161 Why are you frightened? 95
Mark 4:35–41

162 You are with me 95
From Psa. 121

7. When you are worried

163 Look at the crows 96
Luke 12:22–24

164 Why worry? 96
Luke 12:25–26

165 Look at the flowers 96
Luke 12:27–28

166 Don't be upset 96
From Luke 12:29–31

167 Either – or 98
Matt. 6:24

168 Where your heart will be 98
Matt. 6:19–21

169 What's the use? 98
Luke 12:16–21

8. Friends and enemies

170 Friends 99
Eccl. 4:9–10

171 Ecclus. 6:7,14–15 99

172 The start of an argument 99
Proverbs 17:14 and 22:24–25

173 They are for war 100
From Psa. 120

174 My enemies persecute me 100
Psa. 56:1–4,8–11

175 Love your enemies 101
Matt. 5:43–45

176 Do not destroy your enemies 101
From Luke 9:51–56

177 You should have had mercy 102
Matt. 18:23–35

178 How often? 102
Luke 17:3–4

179 So there can be peace 102
From Eph. 4:2–3 and Col. 3:13–15

180 He endured suffering 103
Isa. 53:3,7

181 If you forgive people's sins 104
John 20:19–23

182 With his own body 104
From Eph. 2:14,16–17; and 1 Cor. 1:3; and
Rom. 15:33

9. Sin, repentance and forgiveness

183 Forsaking the spring of fresh water 106
Jer. 2:13

184 They will not give up their sinning 106
From Jer. 9:3–5

185 Filled with wickedness 107
Rom. 1:28–31

186 Their minds are dull 107
Matt. 13:14–15

187 They did not receive Christ 107
John 1:10–11

188 John 3:19–20 107

189 From John 16:8–9 107

190 Joy in heaven 108
Luke 15:1–7

191 Greater than sin 108
From Isa. 57:15–19

192 The angels rejoice 109
Luke 15:8–10

193 He is so good to us 109
From Psa. 103:2–11

194 He ran towards him 110
From Luke 15:11–24

195 You are merciful to all 110
Rom. 2:4

196 From Wis. 11:21–24 110

197 God, have pity on me, a sinner!.... 111
Luke 18:9–14

198 If we confess our sins 111
1 John 1:8–9

199 From Psa. 32:1–5 111

200 Whoever has committed no sin 113
From John 8:3–11

201 Seeking the lost 113
Luke 19:1–10

202 See yourself for what you are 113
Matt. 7:2–5

203 Put on the new self 113
From Eph. 4:22–25,28

204 From Deut. 30:2–3 113

10. God is ahead of us

205 No more than a shadow 114
Psa. 39:5–8

206 Dying 114
From Psa. 90:3–17

207 Is everything useless? 115
From Eccl. 1,2,4,12

208 We wait to be set free 116
Rom. 8:18–23

209 You will be glad 116
John 16:20–22 and Eph. 1:4–8

210 The guarantee 117
1 Cor. 15:12,17,20

211 I am filled with gladness 117
From Acts 2:25–28

212 What he will say 119
Matt. 25:31–40

213 Wait until the harvest 119
Matt. 13:24–30,37–40

214 We shall see him 120
1 Cor. 13:9–10,12

215 John 17:3 120

216 What awaits us 120
1 Cor. 2:9

217 I make all things new 120
Rev. 21:1–5

218 The full nature of God 122
From Col. 1:15–20

Index of Subjects 135

Index of Bible Passages 137

List of Illustrations 139

Index of Subjects

Numbers refer to the sections

Abraham 21–27
Alone 159–60, 162, 166
Anointing 39
Ascension 118
Children of God 13–14, 34, 40, 43–44, 125, 175
Christmas 60–62
Church 124, 128–36
Commandments of God 30–35, 50, 81, 145–50
Covenant with God
– God's covenant with Abraham 22–27
– God's covenant with Jacob 28–29
– God's covenant with Israel 17–21, 45, 50
– The new covenant 50, 104
– Joined to God through Jesus 137–44
Creation 6–7, 19, 36–38, 208, 217–18
David 39–42
Death 205–6, 211
Easter 102–17, 181, 210
Enemies 172–76
Faith
– Abraham's faith 22–27
– Israel's faith 8
– Faith in Jesus Christ 90–91, 101, 116, 136–38, 141, 143, 161, 189
Forgiveness
– God forgives our sins 45, 47, 49–52, 177, 179, 190–201
– Forgiving each other 150, 175, 177–79, 181
Friendship 170–71
God
– His mystery 1–6, 160
– Good and merciful 101, 177, 191, 193, 195–96
– He is with us 9, 17, 19, 20, 162
– Like a father 13, 165, 194
– Like a mother 14, 44

– Like a shepherd 15–16, 190
– Creator 7, 36–38
– Saviour 10–11
– Liberator 8–9, 18, 21
– Lord 7
– Father of Jesus 95, 97, 101, 119, 146
Guilt *See* Sin and guilt
Holy Spirit *See* Spirit of God
Hope 208–11, 214
Jacob 28–29
Jesus
– Christ (Messiah) 60–62, 64–65, 100, 129
– Lord 61–62, 116, 119, 121, 137
– Saviour 61, 176
– Prophet 72, 92, 96, 107, 114
– Head 130, 218
– King 102, 108
– Judge 212–13
– Son of David 90
– Son of God 60, 67, 95, 107, 129, 140
John the Baptist 63–65
Joy
– God's joy 190, 192, 194
– Our joy 20, 59, 117, 127, 134, 209, 211
Kingdom of God 55–57, 78–80, 84–87, 94
Law *See* Commandments of God
Liberation from Egypt 8–11, 18, 21
Listening to God 83, 136, 143, 186
Lord's Prayer 153
Love
– God's love for us 9, 13–14, 18–19, 21, 43–44, 58, 74, 79, 104, 146–48, 193, 195–96
– Our love for God 30–31, 81, 145, 147
– Our love for others 32–35, 77, 81–82, 127, 132, 145, 147–49, 151, 179, 212

Mary 60–62, 75
Messiah
– The anointed King of Israel 39
– The promise of the one to come 49, 52–54
– Jesus the Messiah 60–62, 64–65, 100, 129
Moses 5, 9–10, 12, 18
Pardon *See* Forgiveness
Parents 35
Peace 55–57, 74, 127, 150, 179, 182
Pentecost 122–27
People of God 8, 17–18, 21–22, 44, 48, 50–52, 133
Peter 66, 68, 129
Possessions 167–69
Praise 1–2, 4, 6–7, 11, 20, 36–38, 58, 119, 193, 196, 199

Prayer 152–58
Repentance 43–48, 63, 70, 84–85, 124, 190, 192–99, 201–4
Resurrection 112–17, 181, 210
Sabbath 32, 95
Sin and guilt 42–48, 183–89, 198
Spirit of God 39, 51, 60, 122–27
Suffering
– Of Jesus 105–10, 173, 180
– Of mankind 205–11
Trusting God 16, 159–60, 162, 173–74, 205–6, 211
Will of God 30–35, 37, 50, 81, 145–51
Worry 105, 159, 161–66

Index of Bible Passages

Numbers refer to the sections

Genesis

12:1–4	22
13:14–18	23
15:1–6	24
17:1–8	25
18:1–16	26
21:1–7	27
28:10–19	28
32:22–30	29

Exodus

2:23–24	9
3:1–17	9
14	10
15:1–13	11
16:1–15	12
19:1–8	18
33:18–23	5

Leviticus

19:9–18	33
26:9,11–12	17

Deuteronomy

5:6–21	32
6:4–5	31
7:6–9	21
8:7–10	19
10:12–13	30
26:5–9	8
30:2–3	204

1 Samuel

16:6–13	39
17	41

2 Samuel

11 and 12	42

Psalms

2:7,10–12	40
8	38
13	160
16:8–11	211
23:1–2,4	16
32:1–5	199
39:5–8	205
56:1–4,8–11	174

Psalms (cont.)

89:8–9	2
89:9–17	7
90:2	1
90:3–17	206
103:2–11	193
103:13,17–18	13
104	20
120	173
121	162
139:17–18	4
148	36

Proverbs

17:14	172
20:22	172
22:24–25	172

Ecclesiastes

1:2,4,12	207
4:9–10	170

Isaiah

1:2–4	43
5:1–7	48
6:10	186
9:2–7	54
11:2–4	53
11:6–9	56
25:6–8	57
40:1–5	49
40:10–11	15
40:12,15,17,18	6
49:15	14
53:3,7	180
55:8–9	3
57:15–19	191

Jeremiah

1:4–9,16–19	46
2:13	183
3:12–13	47
9:3–5	184
31:31–34	50

Ezekiel

34:1–6,11,16,23	52
36:26–28	51

Hosea

11:1–5	44
14:2–5	45

Micah

4:3–4	55

Esther

4:17,19	159

Wisdom

9:1–4	37
11:21–24	196

Ecclesiasticus

3:6–8	35
4:1–11	34
6:7,14–15	171

Matthew

2:1–12	62
4:23–5:10	74
5:12–16	135
5:43–45	175
6:5–6	155
6:7–8	154
6:9–13	153
6:19–21	168
6:24	167
7:2–5	202
7:7–11	158
7:16–17	144
7:24–27	143
8:2–3	89
12:30	138
12:33–35	144
13:1–9,18–23	83
13:14–15	186
13:24–30,37–40	213
13:31–32	87
13:33	86
13:44	84
13:45	85
16:13–19	129
18:19–20	157
18:23–35	177
25:31–40	212
28:16–20	128

Mark

1:14–15	70
1:21–22	71
2:1–12	93
3:31–35	75
4:35–41	161
6:1–6	72
7:32–37	88
9:33–37	76
10:13–16	79
10:46–52	90
12:28–34	145
12:41–44	77
16:1–8	113

Luke

1:26–38	60
2:1–18	61
3:1–9	63
4:16–24,28–30	73
5:1–11	68
5:16	152
5:27–32	69
6:12	152
7:1–10	91
7:11–16	92
7:18–22	94
9:51–56	176
10:3,16	136
10:25–28	81
10:29–37	82
11:5–8	156
12:8–9	139
12:16–21	169
12:22–24	163
12:25–26	164
12:27–28	165
12:29–31	166
15:1–7	190
15:8–10	192
15:11–24	194
17:3–4	178
17:20–21	80
18:9–14	197
19:1–10	201
19:28–38	102
22:1–6	103
22:7–20	104
22:24–27	78

22:39–46	105	8:18–23	208
22:47–53	106	12:4–6	131
22:54,63–71	107	13:8–10	151
23:1–11	108	15:33	182
23:13–16,21–24	109		
23:26,32–38,44–46	110	1 Corinthians	
23:50–54	111	1:3	182
24:13–31	114	2:9	216
24:36–43	115	13:9–10,12	214
		15:1–8,20	112
John		15:12,17,20	210
1:10–11	187		
1:19–27	64	2 Corinthians	
1:35–39	65	3:2–3	126
1:40–41	66	5:17–18	141
1:43–50	67		
3:19–20	188	Galatians	
5:1–18	95	5:22,25	127
6:1–15	96		
6:22–69	97	Ephesians	
7:10–12	98	1:3,20–22	119
7:14–16	99	1:4–8	209
7:40–47	100	1:17–18,22–23	130
8:3–11	200	2:14,16–17	182
10:22–39	101	4:2–3	179
13:1–35	149	4:22–25,28	203
14:21–23	146	4:32	150
14:27–28	117		
15:1–5	142	Philippians	
16:8–9	189	2:6–11	121
16:20–22	209		
17:3	215	Colossians	
17:21–22	132	1:15–20	218
20:19–23	181	2:6–7	137
20:24–29	116	3:13–15	179
21:25	120		
		1 Peter	
Acts		2:9–10	133
1:8–11	118	3:9–11	150
2:1–4	122		
2:6–33	123	1 John	
2:25–28	211	1:1–4	59
2:37–38,41–42	124	1:8–9	198
2:44–47	134	4:7–12	148
		4:15	140
Romans		4:19–21	147
1:28–31	185		
2:4	195	Revelation	
8:14–15	125	21:1–5	217

List of Illustrations

Page 3: The hand of God, *c.* 1100 (Herder Picture Library).
Page 5: Erich Lessing Magnum photograph. (The desert of Judah between Jerusalem and Jericho.)
Page 7: Wilhelm Gross, The prophet receives the wisdom of the Lord, wood engraving.
Page 8/9: Toni Schneiders, Lindau.
Page 10: Jürgen Burghartz, linocut.
Page 11: Jürgen Burghartz, linocut.
Page 12: (Left & centre:) Jürgen Burghartz, linocut.
Page 12: (Right:) Richard Seewald, chalk drawing.
Page 13: Erich Lessing Magnum photograph. (Sinai peninsula by the Red Sea.)
Page 14: Richard Seewald, chalk drawing.
Page 15: (Left:) Oswald Kettenberger, Maria Laach.
Page 15: (Right:) Rudolf Dietrich, Munich.
Page 16: Erich Lessing Magnum photograph. (Clay figure of a nomadic shepherd, *c.* 18th century B.C.)
Page 17: Werner Persy, Moses distributes water, wood engraving.
Page 18: Erich Lessing Magnum photograph. (North side of Lake Gennesaret near Bethsaida.)
Page 20: Toni Schneider-Manzell, bronze relief.
Page 22: Jürgen Burghartz, linocut.
Page 23: Emil Wachter, Abraham and the Lord, colour lithographic print.
Page 24: Thomas Höpker, Munich.
Page 25: (Above:) South German Picture Service, Munich.
Page 25: (Below:) South German Picture Service, Munich (Heike Riemer).
Page 26/27: Toni Schneiders, Lindau.
Page 29: Richard Seewald, chalk drawing.
Page 31: The sovereign Lord enthroned, glass window from Strasbourg minster, *c.* 1200 (Herder Picture Library).
Page 32: Gerhard Marcks, Jonah shouting in repentance, wood engraving.
Page 33: Willy Kretzer, Freiburg im Breisgau.
Page 34: Emil Nolde, Head of a prophet, wood engraving.
Page 35: Erich Lessing Magnum photograph.
Page 37: The good shepherd, ivory, *c.* 380 (Herder Picture Library).
Page 39: Herbert Falken, Forecourt and Temple.
Page 41: Head of Jesus (see page 63).
Page 42: Annunciation, miniature from the sacramentary of St. Gereon, Cologne, *c.* 1000.
Page 43: Joachim Schuster.
Page 44: Adoration, wooden door of St. Maria im Kapitol, Cologne, *c.* 1065 (Herder Picture Library).
Page 45: Matthias Grünewald, Isenheim altar, *c.* 1513, Kolmar (Herder Picture Library).

Page 46/47: Erich Lessing Magnum photograph. (Lake Gennesaret seen from the north-west.)
Page 48: Christ the teacher with open scroll, ivory, *c.* 380 (Herder Picture Library).
Page 49: Josef Hegenbarth.
Page 51: Reinhard Herrmann, biblical frieze.
Page 52: Gerhard Kraaz, Brotherly love, Indian-ink drawing.
Page 53: Herder Picture Library.
Page 54: (Left & right:) Erich Lessing Magnum photograph.
Page 55: Erich Lessing Magnum photograph.
Page 56: Hans-Joachim Burgert, The healing of the blind man.
Page 58: The healing of the paralysed man, miniature, second half of the 12th century (Erich Lessing Magnum photograph).
Page 59: (Left:) The healing of the leper (see also page 58).
Page 59: (Right:) The healing of the blind man (see also page 58).
Page 61: Multiplying the bread, miniature from the Golden Gospel Book of Echternach, *c.* 990 (Herder Picture Library).
Page 63: Head of Jesus, ivory relief, 11th century (Erich Lessing Magnum photograph).
Page 64: Entry into Jerusalem, wooden door of St. Maria im Kapitol, Cologne, *c.* 1065 (Herder Picture Library).
Page 65: Emil Nolde, Supper (Nolde Foundation).
Page 66: (Left & right:) Josef Hegenbarth.
Page 67: Josef Hegenbarth.
Page 68: Joachim Schuster.
Page 69: A rock tomb on the eastern slope of the Mount of Olives in Jerusalem, which can be shut by rolling a stone across the entrance. (Erich Lessing Magnum photograph.)
Page 70: The women at the tomb, bronze relief from the Bernward door in Hildesheim cathedral, *c.* 1015 (Herder Picture Library).
Page 71: Karl Schmitt-Rottluff, The road to Emmaus, wood engraving.
Page 72/73: The meal at Emmaus, end of the 12th century (Erich Lessing Magnum photograph).
Page 75: Christ as king on the cross, wooden sculpture, Westphalian school, *c.* 1200.
Page 77: Alfred Manessier, Hallelujah, colour lithographic print (© ADAGP Paris and COSMOPRESS Geneva 1975).
Page 78: Christ sends the Spirit, miniature from the lectionary of Cluny, probably 11th century (Herder Picture Library).
Page 79: Emil Wachter.
Page 80: Christ sends out the disciples, miniature from a book of pericopae of Heinrich II, *c.* 1010 (Herder Picture Library).

Page 81: Toni Schneider-Manzell, Simon Peter – do you love me?, bronze relief.
Page 82: Lydia Blöhm, *Gloria Patris*, linocut.
Page 84: The risen Christ has a meal with his disciples. A painting from a crucifix in Pisa, 12th century (Herder Picture Library).
Page 85: Christ the vine, an icon from Siebenbürgen (Willy Pragher).
Page 86: (Left:) Toni Schneiders, Lindau.
Page 86: (Right:) Herder Picture Library.
Page 87: (Left:) Ullstein Picture Service, Berlin (Molodovsky).
Page 87: (Right:) South German Picture Service, Munich.
Page 89: Richard Seewald, chalk drawing.
Page 92: Max Beckmann, Jesus in the desert, lithographic print.
Page 94: Wolfgang Kunz, Hamburg.
Page 95: Toni Schneider-Manzell, bronze relief.
Page 96: South German Picture Service, Munich (Fritz Neuwirth).
Page 97: Erich Lessing Magnum photograph.
Page 98: South German Picture Service, Munich.
Page 99: Kindermann Press Picture Service, Berlin.
Page 100: Hieronymus Bosch (c. 1450–1516), Bearing the cross.
Page 101: foto present, Essen (Volkmer).
Page 103: Otto Pankok, Scoffing, colour wood engraving.
Page 104: The risen Christ appears to the disciples, wooden door of St. Maria im Kapitol, Cologne, c. 1065 (Herder Picture Library).
Page 105: Gerhard Marcks, tympanum of the bronze door in the Marktkirche in Hanover (Herder Picture Library).
Page 106: Herder Picture Library.
Page 108: Joachim Schuster.
Page 109: Joachim Schuster.

Page 110: Karl Schmitt-Rottluff, The prodigal son, wood engraving.
Page 111: Maria Braun, Pharisee and tax collector, wood engraving.
Page 112: Joachim Schuster.
Page 114: South German Picture Service, Munich (Alfred A. Haase).
Page 115: Erich Heckel, colour wood engraving.
Page 116: South German Picture Service, Munich (W. Storto).
Page 117: Toni Schneider-Manzell, bronze relief.
Page 118: (Above:) Christ as Lord of the cosmos, relief on the façade of the cathedral in Assisi, 12th century (Toni Schneiders).
Page 118: (Below:) The six works of compassion combined in three scenes, in the Vatican, c. 1240 (Herder Picture Library).
Page 121: Richard Seewald, chalk drawing.
Page 123: The enthroned Christ, copper-plated, Limoges, 13th century (Erich Lessing Magnum photograph).
Page 142/143: C. E. Bush
Illustration on the front cover: *Christ*, mosaic from St. Apollinare Nuovo in Ravenna (photograph by Erich Lessing).
Illustration on the back cover: Alfred Manessier, *Halleluja*, colour lithograph (copyright © ADAGP Paris and COSMOPRESS Geneva 1975).
We are grateful to all those who have given permission to reproduce illustrations. The bronze reliefs of Toni Schneider-Manzell (pages 20, 81, 95, 117) are to be found on the new door of Speyer Cathedral, photographs by the Rhineland-Pfalz State Picture Agency (Bruno Fischer), published in Philipp Weindel, *The Bronze Door of Speyer Cathedral*, Pilger-Verlag (Speyer 1974).

Jerusalem, the Holy City,
shining with the glory of God.

Revelation 21:10-11

First published in Great Britain 1979

Originally published in the German Federal Republic under the title *Grundschulbibel*, compiled by Günther Weber, © Verlag Herder KG, Freiburg im Breisgau, 1975

British Edition edited by Richard Herkes © Lutterworth Press 1979

The publishers wish to express their gratitude to the Bible Society for their kind permission to reproduce passages (Old and New Testaments) from *The Bible in Today's English Version* (*Good News Bible*) © American Bible Society 1976; and to Messrs. Darton, Longman & Todd Ltd. for permission to reproduce passages (Esther, Wisdom, and Ecclesiasticus) from the *Jerusalem Bible* © Darton, Longman & Todd Ltd. and Doubleday & Company Inc. 1966.

Published by The Westminster Press ®
Philadelphia, Pennsylvania

Printed in Hong Kong

9 8 7 6 5 4 3 2 1